RAND

Student Achievement and the Changing American Family

David W. Grissmer, Sheila Nataraj Kirby,
Mark Berends, Stephanie Williamson

Supported by the
Lilly Endowment Inc.

**Institute on
Education and Training**

RAND's Institute on Education and Training conducts policy analysis to help improve education and training for all Americans.

The Institute examines *all* forms of education and training that people may get during their lives. These include formal schooling from preschool through college; employer-provided training (civilian and military); post-graduate education; proprietary trade schools; and the informal learning that occurs in families, in communities, and with exposure to the media. Reexamining the field's most basic premises, the Institute goes beyond the narrow concerns of each component to view the education and training enterprise as a whole. It pays special attention to how the parts of the enterprise affect one another and how they are shaped by the larger environment. The Institute:

- examines the performance of the education and training system

- analyzes problems and issues raised by economic, demographic, and national security trends

- evaluates the impact of policies on broad, systemwide concerns

- helps decisionmakers formulate and implement effective solutions.

To ensure that its research affects policy and practice, the Institute conducts outreach and disseminates findings to policymakers, educators, researchers, and the public. It also trains policy analysts in the field of education.

RAND is a private, nonprofit institution, incorporated in 1948, which engages in nonpartisan research and analysis on problems of national security and the public welfare. The Institute builds on RAND's long tradition—interdisciplinary, empirical research held to the highest standards of quality, objectivity, and independence.

There is considerable debate in our society and in the research community about the direction and causes of changes in student performance over the last 25 years: whether student performance is getting better or worse, whether the dramatic changes in family and racial/ethnic characteristics have affected average student achievement, and whether the greatly expanded investment in education and other social programs and policies directed toward equal educational opportunities were effective in improving student performance.

These questions are among the most important public policy issues affecting our society's future. The proficiencies and future performance of our children will be partly responsible for our competitive economic position in the world economy. In addition, children's outcomes will partly determine how much future public spending will be required to pay for such programs as prisons and the criminal justice system, welfare, unemployment, and job training, as well as health expenditures arising from treatment of addictions and victims of violent crimes.

Better answers to these questions would help determine how to more effectively allocate the approximately $275–$325 billion of public resources for K–12 education and social programs directed to support families and improve student outcomes. Answers to these basic questions would also help establish whether fundamental school reform is needed and, if so, help provide directions for reform of schools and school financing.

The effectiveness of public policies and investments directed toward children cannot be evaluated without accounting for the changing characteristics and demographics of the American family. Many believe that the family has deteriorated in its capacity to support the development of children. They point to rising levels of single-parent families and working mothers, a greater proportion of children in poverty households, and a higher incidence of births among young, unmarried mothers.

Besides changes in family characteristics, the proportion of children from Hispanic and Asian backgrounds has increased markedly over the last 25 years, mainly due to immigration. There has also been a more gradual increase in the proportion of children who are black. These changing demographic trends also can affect average student performance. If family and demographic characteristics are key factors related to changes in average student achievement, then they must be taken into account before attempting to evaluate the effectiveness of increases in public investments and changing public policies.

In this study, we first estimate the effect that changing family characteristics and race/ethnicity of students would be expected to have on national mathematics and verbal/reading achievement score trends of 14–18-year-old youth between 1970/1975 and 1990. Second, we compare these estimated effects from changing family/demographic characteristics to actual trends in national achievement scores to see how much of the actual trend might be accounted for by changing families and demographics. Third, we estimate the residual effect that cannot be accounted for by family/demographic trends and offer several hypotheses that might help explain the patterns of the residual effects.

This report is intended for government policymakers, educators, researchers, parents, and taxpayers interested in how to effectively and efficiently foster higher student achievement. Research support to build the database used in this analysis was provided jointly by RAND's Institute on Education and Training (IET) through a grant from the Lilly Endowment Inc. and by the Office of the Assistant Secretary of Defense (P&R). The Department of Defense is the nation's largest employer of youth, and as such is vitally concerned with changing levels of achievement among the nation's youth. The results and policy implications of our research are being documented in two separate reports: one for those primarily concerned with domestic issues, and the other focusing mainly on concerns of defense policymakers. The results for domestic audiences are summarized in MR-535-LE, *Student Achievement and the Changing American Family: An Executive Summary.* This report was written under the aegis of the IET.

CONTENTS

FIGURES

TABLES

SUMMARY

BACKGROUND AND PURPOSE OF THE STUDY

There is a continuing national debate on the quality of our children's family environment, the quality of their schools, and how changes in families and schools may be affecting the level of student achievement. Within this debate, questions remain about whether public policies and increased investments in education and social programs are effective in improving student achievement. In addition, as the student population becomes more racially and ethnically diverse, there is growing concern about the inequality of educational outcomes between minority and nonminority students.

Motivating these concerns are negative perceptions about achievement trends, the changing family environment, and the effectiveness of social programs and public education. Specifically, these include the following:

- A perceived decline in student achievement as measured by scores on the widely publicized Scholastic Aptitude Test (SAT).

- A perceived deterioration in the family environment, with particular emphasis on four trends: increase in the number of teen mothers and out-of-wedlock births, increase in the number of children living in poverty, increase in the proportion of mothers working, and increase in the number of children living in single-parent families.

- The perceived ineffectiveness of the very large increases in the real per-pupil K–12 educational expenditures and other social programs over the last 25 years in producing higher student achievement.

Trying to sort out the relative contributions of families, schools, and social programs to student achievement is a complex exercise, for several reasons. First, there are conflicting trends in student achievement, depending on which tests are used, and a great deal of caution needs to be observed in selecting a representative test and in interpreting its results. Second, explaining trends is difficult because several factors perceived to affect student achievement have all changed dramatically: the family environment, demographic mix of students, school quality, public policies directed toward providing equal educational opportunity, and public investment in schools and social programs. Third, assessing the effect of public policies and investment is problematic partly because empirical evidence indicates that family and demographic changes probably have the largest effects on test scores; thus, family/demographic effects on student achievement need to be estimated before making assessments of the effect of public policies and investment.

These substantial changes—in family and demographic characteristics of students, the initiatives to provide equal educational opportunity through such policies as integration of public schools and bilingual education programs, and the increased public investment in schools and social programs—all combine to make the last 25 years a unique period in our history and provide a unique opportunity to understand the trends in student achievement and their causes. Understanding how our families and schools have changed, the impact of these changes on student performance, and whether public policies and investment make a difference will help provide answers to some of the most important public policy questions affecting the future of our society.

Answering such questions and sorting out the relative contributions of the various factors to student achievement is the main purpose of this overall project. The present study primarily focuses on estimating the change in achievement test scores that can be attributed to changing family and demographic characteristics. Family characteristics included in the analysis are family income, family size, parental education levels, age of mother at child's birth, labor-force participation of the mother, and single-parent families. Our analysis estimates the expected effects that changing family environment and demographic characteristics would have had on the student achievement scores of a national sample of students ages 14–18 between 1970/1975 and 1990. The direction of the predicted effects of these family changes on test scores can provide evidence on whether the family environment in 1990 is more or less supportive of student achievement compared with the environment of similarly aged students in 1970/1975. If we predict a decline in scores due to family changes, this would reinforce the common perception that the family environment has indeed deteriorated over this time period; a predicted increase in scores would indicate more supportive family characteristics and environment in 1990.

We compare our *predicted* changes in test scores from family/demographic changes to *actual* changes in achievement scores of national samples of youth from 1970/1975 to 1990 in order to gauge the effect of factors other than family and demographic characteristics on student achievement. If the residual between actual changes in test scores and predicted changes based on family/demographic effects alone is positive, then this would suggest that other factors had a positive effect on test scores, while a negative residual would suggest the opposite.

Two major factors that could help account for a positive residual between actual score changes and those accounted for by family/demographic changes are (a) changing public policies in the area of equal educational opportunity and increased levels of public investment in schools and children, and (b) changing productivity of schools. The residual can provide some evidence about whether effects from public policy and public investment and changing schools are present.

To help determine if the pattern of residual differences is consistent or inconsistent with positive effects from public policies, public investment, and schools, we estimate family effects and residual differences for black, Hispanic, and non-Hispanic white youth. It is possible that minority and nonminority families may have changed in different ways over this period and that the predicted family effects differ across these groups. In addition, the effects of public policies and investment would not be the same across racial/ethnic groups because public policies concerning equal opportunity and additional public investment in education and social programs were differentially targeted toward minority and/or lower-income families, children, and school districts. Thus, we might expect the indicators of these effects to be larger for minority groups. As such, our analysis provides separate estimates of family effects, the predicted change in test scores based on these family effects, and the gap between actual and predicted test score changes for blacks, Hispanics, and non-Hispanic whites.

METHODOLOGY

The methodology consists of three steps: (1) developing quantitative models linking student achievement to family and demographic characteristics; (2) using these models to predict test scores for a national sample of children using their family and demographic characteristics from 1970, 1975, and 1990; and (3) comparing the mean changes in these predicted test scores between 1970/1975 and 1990 (changes due to family and demographic characteristics) to actual changes in test scores of a national sample of children and estimating a residual not accounted for by family/demographic factors. This pattern of residuals can provide initial evidence that additional factors—hypothesized to be primarily changes in schools, public policies, and public investment—may have affected student achievement.

Step 1: Estimating How Much Family and Demographic Characteristics Affect Test Scores

We first estimate models linking test scores to family and demographic characteristics; we have used two quite different nationally representative samples of adolescents. The datasets are the National Longitudinal Survey of Youth (NLSY), 1980, from which we selected students aged 15–18 years, and the National Education Longitudinal Survey (NELS), 1988, which samples eighth graders. The dependent variables in the models are the standardized scores for mathematics and verbal/reading tests that were administered to all children in the samples. Test scores are assumed to be a function of a set of independent family and demographic variables that are common to both surveys. These include family income, family structure (single-parent or two-parent households), family size, parental education, labor-force participation of the mother, age of the mother at child's birth, and race/ethnicity. These are the primary family variables that have changed over the last 20 years and have been linked to student achievement.

Step 2: Estimating How Much Changing Families and Demographics Between 1970/1975 and 1990 Would Change Test Scores

These equations are then used to predict test scores at the individual level for a representative sample of U.S. children of similar ages in 1970, 1975, and 1990, extracted from the March Current Population Surveys. We compute the mean shift of the distribution of test scores from 1970/1975 to 1990 to provide an overall measure of the *net* effect of changing family and demographic characteristics on test scores. We make black/nonblack comparisons using the 1970 and 1990 data; comparisons for three racial/ethnic groups—non-Hispanic whites, Hispanics, and blacks—are done using the 1975 and 1990 predicted test scores.[1]

Step 3: Estimating How Much Changing Family and Demographic Characteristics Can Account for Actual Test Score Changes

The third step is to compare the changes in test scores predicted from changes in family and demographic characteristics to actual changes in national test scores. Although SAT scores are probably what the public most often uses to form opinions about national test score trends, these scores are seriously flawed as indicators of how the average achievement of American students is changing, for several reasons (Koretz, 1986). First, the SAT sample is not a representative sample of U.S. students. Second, the sample contains a constantly changing proportion and composition of students, and this has introduced a downward bias in scores over time. Third, from our perspective, a more serious flaw is that the SAT sample excludes students not going to college. As evidence cited below indicates, the

---

[1]We limit ourselves to black/nonblack comparisons for the 1970–1990 period because the Current Population Survey does not identify Hispanics in 1970.

largest changes in scores over the last 20 years have probably occurred among lower-scoring students, who are less likely to go to college or to take the SAT. Thus, the SAT scores probably missed the students making the largest changes.

The National Assessment of Educational Progress (NAEP) is a set of standardized tests that has been given by the Department of Education since the early 1970s to a nationally representative sample of students aged 9, 13, and 17 years. The questions used for comparisons over time have not changed and thus can be used for making comparisons of student achievement over time. These tests provide the best data to monitor the achievement trends of U.S. students over the last 25 years. We compare the NLSY results for 15–18-year-old youth to NAEP scores for 17-year-olds and the NELS results for eighth graders to NAEP scores for 13-year-olds. These comparisons allow us to calculate what proportion of the actual score changes can be attributed to family/demographic changes and what remains to be explained by other factors.

RESULTS

The analysis and evidence reported here support a more positive picture than is usually drawn of the achievement of American students aged 14–18 years, the capacity of American families to support that achievement, and the effectiveness of public policies and public investment.

How Much Do Family and Demographic Characteristics Affect Test Scores?

The results from the NELS and NLSY both show large differences in test scores for family/demographic characteristics and great similarity in the direction and relative significance of these differences. Figure S.1 shows simple comparisons of mathematics test scores[2]

---

[2]The mathematics and verbal/reading test score differences show fairly similar patterns and sizes of differences.

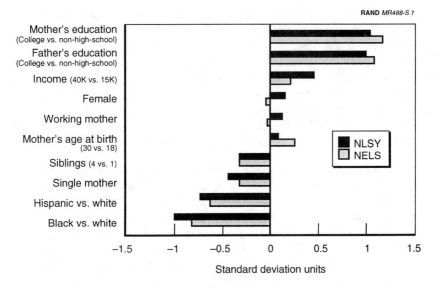

Figure S.1—Simple Differences in Mean Mathematics Test Scores for
Selected Groups, NLSY and NELS

among youth in different types of families from the NLSY and NELS.[3]
The figure shows large differences among the average test scores of
children living in families with different levels of parental education
or of different racial/ethnic background. For instance, a child whose
mother or father graduated from college scores approximately 1.0
standard deviation higher than a child whose mother or father did
not graduate from high school, while black and Hispanic youth score
from 0.50 to 1.0 of a standard deviation lower than non-Hispanic
white youth.

Somewhat smaller test score differences are evident among young
people living in families with different levels of annual income

---

[3]We utilize a consistent measure—proportion of a standard deviation—throughout to
measure differences in test scores. Another measure commonly used in reporting test
scores is the percentile. This shows the relative standing of a particular score and
measures the proportion of children scoring lower than that score. A 0.10 of a standard deviation difference in test scores is approximately 3.4 percentile points for most
children. So two groups of children whose average scores differ by 0.10 of a standard
deviation would indicate that one group scores—on average—3.4 percentile points
higher than the other group.

($40,000 versus $15,000), families of different size (four siblings versus one sibling), families having older or younger mothers (age 30 at birth versus age 18), and two-parent versus single-parent families. For instance, children living in two-parent families score about 0.30 to 0.40 of a standard deviation higher than those in single-parent families, while children in large families score approximately 0.30 of a standard deviation lower than children from smaller families. There is little difference in test scores between those with working mothers and those with nonworking mothers.

Public debate and the press often focus on these simple comparisons of achievement scores for different family and demographic characteristics and mistakenly attribute the difference in scores between two groups to the particular characteristic in which the groups differ. Such inferences are misleading, however, because the students being compared usually differ in several characteristics, not just the one being cited. For instance, young people in higher-income families are also more likely to have parents with higher levels of education and to be nonminority. Thus, the difference in average test scores between children from high-income families and those from low-income families is probably due to a combination of factors, not just income alone. A better measure of the effect of income on test scores is a controlled comparison of two groups of young people who have similar family characteristics except for income. This is true for other characteristics as well.

Figure S.2 summarizes these controlled comparison differences for mathematics scores.[4]

This figure shows that the net effect of each factor is considerably smaller than the simple comparisons in Figure S.1. However, the controlled differences remain significant for certain characteristics. For example, youth whose parents are college graduates score about 0.50 of a standard deviation higher than youth who are otherwise similar but have parents who did not graduate from high school. In

---

[4]These effects are derived by using the estimates from our multivariate model of student achievement. Multivariate models allow us to examine the effect of a particular characteristic, *holding constant other important variables.*

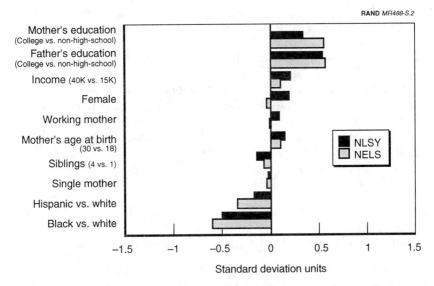

Figure S.2—Net Differences in Mean Mathematics Test Scores for
Selected Groups, NLSY and NELS

addition, controlling for other family characteristics, the difference
between blacks and non-Hispanic whites is 0.50 of a standard deviation, and the difference between Hispanics and non-Hispanic whites
is somewhat smaller. Youth with different levels of family income or
different family sizes show much smaller differences in test scores.
Controlled test score differences due to family structure and labor-
force participation of the mother appear to be negligible. These results suggest that the simple differences between youth scores in
single- and two-parent families arise directly from other differences
in family characteristics, such as family income, parental education,
or family size, rather than the structure of the one-parent versus two-
parent family itself.

How Much Would Changing Families and Demographics Change Test Scores?

We use the estimates from the multivariate models (which formed
the basis for Figure S.2 above) to predict the changes in test scores
that would be expected due to the changes in family and

demographic characteristics that occurred between 1970/1975 and 1990.

We find that 14–18-year-olds living in U.S. families in 1990 would be predicted to score *higher,* not lower, on tests compared to youth in families in 1970. The size of the shift in mean scores is approximately 0.20 of a standard deviation. This means that youth in 1990 would be expected to have scores about 7 percentile points higher than their counterparts in 1970, based on combined changes in demographic and family characteristics. It should be emphasized that these findings estimate *average* effects when taking account of all American families with 14–18-year-olds.

Our analysis suggests that the most important family influences on student test scores are the level of parental education, family size, family income, and the age of the mother when the child was born.

Of these variables, the two that have changed most dramatically in a favorable direction are parental education levels and family size. Children in 1990 are living with better-educated parents and in smaller families. These factors are the primary reasons that changes in family characteristics would predict higher test scores. For example, 7 percent of mothers of 15–18-year-old children in 1970 were college graduates, compared to 16 percent in 1990, whereas 38 percent did not have high school degrees in 1970, compared to only 17 percent in 1990. Similar, but somewhat smaller, changes occurred in the educational attainment of fathers. Changes in family size were also dramatic. Only about 48 percent of 15–18-year-old children lived in families with at most one sibling in 1970, compared to 73 percent in 1990.

Our analysis indicates that average family income changed little over the period 1970 to 1990 (in real terms), so it would not be expected to affect average test scores. However, the decline in family size coupled with unchanged average family income mean that family income per child actually increased from 1970 to 1990.

One change that has had a slight negative effect on test scores is the small decline in the average age of the mother at the child's birth. This is due partly to increased births to younger mothers, but also to the decline in family size, which reduces the number of children born to older mothers.

The effect of the large increase in working mothers and single-parent families is more complex (discussed in more detail below). Our equations imply that the large increase in working mothers would— other things equal—have a negligible or small positive effect on youth test scores. However, the mother's labor-force participation is measured when the youth was approximately 14 years old, so our results may not apply to younger children.

In the case of the increase in single mothers, our models imply no negative effects from the changed family structure *alone*. However, such families tend to have much lower income levels, so the predictions for youth in these families incorporate a negative impact due to increasing numbers of poor, single-parent families.

We turn now to the results by racial/ethnic group between 1975 and 1990. Figures S.3 (mathematics) and S.4 (verbal) show the estimated family effects separately for non-Hispanic whites, blacks, and Hispanics as well as the total youth population between 1975 and 1990. Higher mathematics scores in 1990 would be expected for 14–15 and

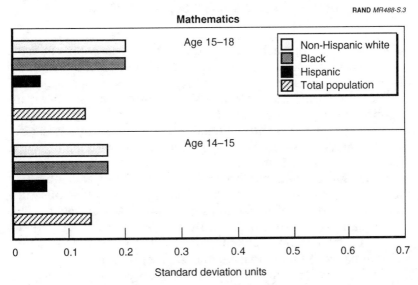

Figure S.3—Estimated Family and Demographic Effects on Mathematics Test Scores Between 1975 and 1990 by Racial/Ethnic Group

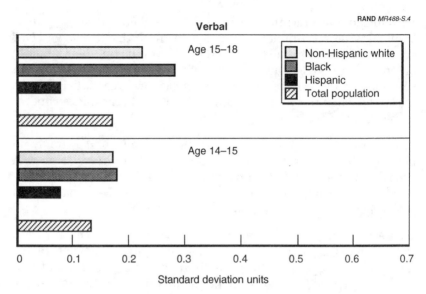

Figure S.4—Estimated Family and Demographic Effects on Verbal Test
Scores Between 1975 and 1990 by Racial/Ethnic Group

15–18-year-olds for each racial/ethnic group based on changing
family characteristics. The data show that non-Hispanic white and
black youth have similar predicted family gains of approximately
0.20 of a standard deviation, but Hispanic youth show smaller gains
of approximately 0.05 of a standard deviation. Verbal/reading score
comparisons show slightly higher gains than comparisons for
mathematics, although the pattern is similar by racial/ethnic groups.
The positive changes in the black family in terms of increased
parental education and reduced family size are actually greater than
those for non-Hispanic white families, but there were offsetting
increases in births to younger and single mothers. The smaller gains
for Hispanic youth are explained by smaller increases in parental
education, falling family income, and smaller reductions in family
size compared to that of black families. This is probably due to the
continuing immigration of large numbers of Hispanic families into
the population, many of whom may have lower levels of educational
achievement and fewer labor-market skills than previous waves of
immigrants (Borjas, 1990).

How Much of Test Score Changes Can Be Accounted for by Changes in Family and Demographics?

We compare our projected family/demographic effects on test scores to actual trends in NAEP test scores over similar time periods and for similar age groups to see how much of the actual changes might plausibly be attributed to changes in family/demographic characteristics. We first look at the trends in NAEP test scores. Figures S.5 and S.6 show NAEP score differences by racial/ethnic group between 1975 and 1990 for 13- and 17-year-old students. The results show *gains* in actual scores on both mathematics and verbal/reading for 13- and 17-year-old students for each racial/ethnic group. These findings are not unique to this study but have been reported previously by several other researchers.

The NAEP gains for black and Hispanic students are significantly larger than those for non-Hispanic white students on each test for both 13- and 17-year-old students. Gains are from 0.45 to 0.65 of a standard deviation for black students, 0.15 to 0.50 of a standard deviation for Hispanics, and around 0.00 to 0.15 for non-Hispanic

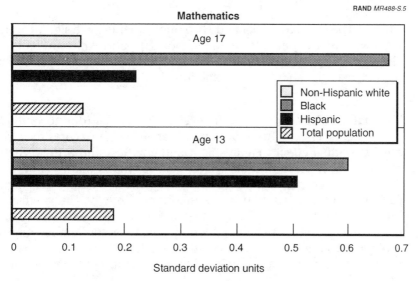

Figure S.5—Change in NAEP Mathematics Scores by Racial/Ethnic Group Between 1978 and 1990 for 13- and 17-Year-Old Students

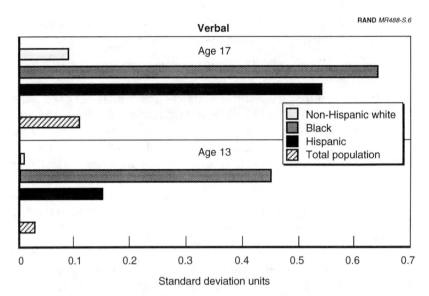

Figure S.6—Change in NAEP Verbal Scores by Racial/Ethnic Group
Between 1975 and 1990 for 13- and 17-Year-Old Students

whites. The gains for black and Hispanic students have significantly narrowed the gap between them and non-Hispanic white students—although a large gap remains. Figures S.7 (mathematics) and S.8 (verbal/reading) show these reductions in the test score gap among racial/ethnic groups.

We subtracted the predicted change in test scores (due to family/ demographic effects) from the actual change in NAEP scores to compute a residual effect. Figures S.9 (mathematics) and S.10 (verbal/ reading) show these residuals. The data for mathematics show no residual gain for non-Hispanic white students, indicating that their gains in test scores could be accounted for entirely by family effects. But there are large positive residuals for Hispanics and black students, suggesting that changing family characteristics alone cannot explain the large gains made by these students. In fact, changing family characteristics account for only about a third of the total gain.

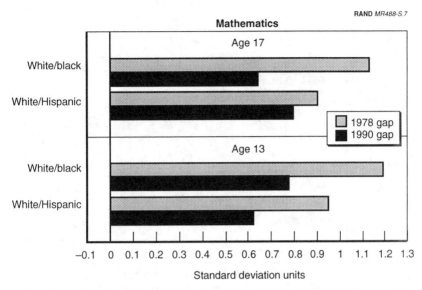

Figure S.7—Comparison of Differences Between Racial/Ethnic Groups in NAEP Mathematics Scores in 1978 and 1990

For verbal/reading scores, the data generally indicate smaller residual gains than for mathematics, but still show substantial black and Hispanic residual gains not accounted for by family effects. The verbal/reading data also show that non-Hispanic white students have a small negative residual for both age groups, indicating that their NAEP gains were not as large as would be expected from family changes.

DISCUSSION OF RESULTS AND FUTURE RESEARCH

The American Family

We have used a single measure—test scores—to view the effects on youth of changes in the family. While other measures of children's development may show different results, this measure provides no evidence of a deteriorating family environment for youth who were 14–18 in 1990 compared to youth who were 14–18 in 1970/1975. Since family influence starts early in a child's life and probably has a

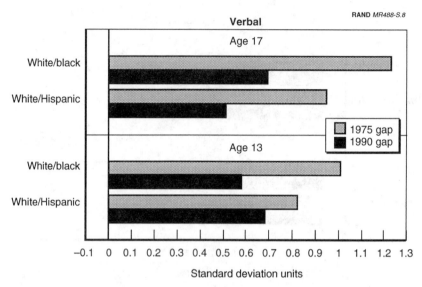

Figure S.8—Comparison of Differences Between Racial/Ethnic Groups
in NAEP Verbal Scores in 1975 and 1990

cumulative impact, the analysis essentially compares families from the late 1950s and 1960s to those from the 1970s and 1980s. Although dramatic changes have occurred in the characteristics of American families in this period—some positive, some negative—attention has focused almost exclusively on the changes perceived to be detrimental to children. The families in 1990 have more highly educated parents with fewer children and similar levels of family income compared to the families in 1970/1975. These characteristics are strongly related to student achievement and are the primary reason for predicted test score gains due to changes in family/demographic characteristics.

Although our results show that average real family income changed little over this period, this average masks two significant changes. Family income has been maintained for many two-parent families only by having two wage earners, and family income declined significantly for many children in going from a two-parent to a single-parent family. However, other characteristics of a family can

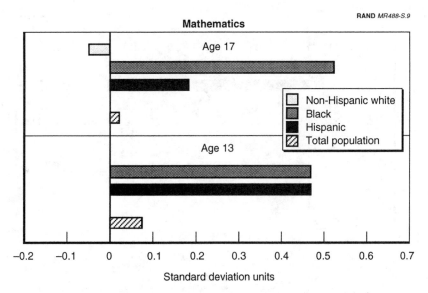

Figure S.9—Residual Difference Between NAEP and Family Effects on
Mathematics Test Scores for Different Racial/Ethnic Groups, 1978–1990

be changed when a transition is made from a two-parent to a single-parent family or from a nonworking to a working mother. For instance, these decisions can change attained educational levels, family size, and the timing of births. So the interpretation of the effects of increased numbers of working mothers and single-parent families must take account of their indirect effects on other variables as well as direct effects.

Our analysis accounts for these indirect effects of increased numbers of working mothers and single-parent families as well as direct effects. Our results indicate that the direct effects on achievement are very small from increased numbers of working mothers and single-parent families.

The lack of a direct effect from the structure of a single-parent family is a little surprising. However, this may partly be explained by previous but unmeasured conditions that existed for children currently in single-parent families when they were in their original two-parent family. For instance, sustained marital conflict, often

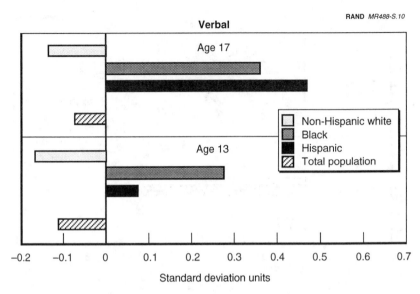

Figure S.10—Residual Difference Between NAEP and Family Effects on
Verbal Test Scores for Different Racial/Ethnic Groups, 1975–1990

involving children, can occur before divorce. Sustained conflict within a family can significantly affect children's development, and children who live in single-parent families resulting from divorce are probably much more likely to have been exposed to this detrimental environment in their original family. Thus, for these children, the transition to a single-parent family may not have direct negative consequences and, in some cases, might even create a better developmental environment. Thus, the lack of a direct effect on achievement—once other family differences are accounted for—from being in a single-parent family cannot be extrapolated to imply that children who live in a nonconflictual or positive two-parent environment would do as well in a single-family environment.

Our analysis focuses on changes in families with children aged 14–18 between 1970 and 1990. Some believe that the family environment may have worsened for younger children, particularly during the last ten years. There is some evidence to suggest that actual test score gains and estimated family effects are smaller for younger age groups and for more recent time periods (1980–1990). Further research is ongoing to see if the conclusions in this report are also true for younger children (age 6–10) over the same time period, and whether trends and effects are changing in more recent periods.

Test Scores as Indicators of School Quality

Comparisons of simple, unadjusted test scores from one year to the next or across different schools or districts do not provide a valid indicator of the performance of the teachers, schools, or school districts unless the differences in scores are very large compared to what might be accounted for by changing demographic or family characteristics. This is rarely the case; so, any use of unadjusted test scores to judge or reward teachers or schools will inevitably misjudge which teachers and schools are performing better. Indeed, the evidence provided here hints that a stronger case could be made that teachers and schools with large numbers of minority students may have been responsible for the most significant gains in test scores over the last 20 years, while family effects—not schools—may have been responsible for gains in nonminority scores. Although more research is needed to test these hypotheses, this evidence illustrates the possibility of dramatic changes in perspective that more detailed analyses can provide.

Likewise, simple unadjusted nationwide test scores can be misleading as a basis for judging school quality, even if the statistical sample of students taking the tests represents the U.S. student population. Since family and demographic effects can affect scores as well as schools, the test score trends need to be adjusted for such effects before preliminary judgments are made about schools.

As pointed out by others, using the SAT scores as a "report card on American education" is even more tenuous, since the SAT does not even draw a valid statistical sample of U.S. students. The test and samples of students taking it were never designed to provide indicators of national trends in achievement or quality of schools, or provide a report card on American education. Moreover, the two flaws in the statistical sample—an expanding proportion and changing composition of high school students taking the test and exclusion of non-college-bound students—both bias the test scores downward. Excluding the non-college-bound students means that the SAT misses those students making the largest gains over the last 25 years.

The purpose of the SAT test is to improve the college admissions process by providing scores that are comparable across individual students. As long as comparisons are restricted to individual students, the test can provide useful information about students applying to college. However, any aggregation of test scores above the level of the individual student—by high school, school district, state, or the nation—is simply uninterpretable as a measure of student achievement trends or of quality differences among schools, school districts, or states.

An unfortunate fact is that the public perception of school quality is partly shaped by the ever-available, but flawed, SAT scores. SAT scores can strongly influence public perceptions because they are more familiar, repeated frequently, have salience to people's lives, and often support existing opinions. Reporting of aggregated, unadjusted SAT scores for high schools, districts, states, or the nation appears not only to serve no useful public purpose, but to confuse and detract from what should be a well-informed public debate about our families, schools, and students. Terminating the publication of unadjusted aggregated SAT scores might also give more emphasis and resources to the more statistically accurate national tests.

Improving Data for Resource Allocation in Education and Social Policy

Significantly better estimates of family, school, community, and social policy effects on test scores could be obtained if there were one dataset that regularly gave national tests and collected associated data from students, parents, schools, and communities. Although the NELS and NLSY data include this information, they do not provide trend data over time.[5] Such data could be collected through an expanded NAEP data-collection effort, with greater information about parents, students, schools, communities, and district and state educational policies. A companion NAEP sample that starts with younger children and follows them longitudinally also seems

---

[5]Data from the Department of Education make it possible to analyze the senior samples of the National Longitudinal Study of the High School Class of 1972 (NLS-72) and the 1992 wave of the NELS. These datasets have comparable data on test scores and family, school, and community characteristics.

essential for better evaluation of specific interventions and modeling of the rate of learning for individual children over time. These changes would require significant restructuring of the NAEP design as well as a significant new data-collection effort entailing significant increases in costs.

However, such data collected over time could provide trend data for almost all key variables that affect test scores of school-aged children. The result would be that changes in test scores could be more reliably related to changes in families, schools, communities, children's health, and district and state educational policies The longitudinal component starting with younger children and larger samples of at-risk children would support much better evaluation of intervention programs as well as a much better understanding of the origins of poor school performance.

Better data and research not only help families make better educational decisions, but such data can support a much better allocation of the $300 billion or more of public funds spent annually on K–12 education and on family, social, and community programs. The additional funding required to significantly expand the NAEP would pale in comparison to what could be saved through improved private and public resource-allocation decisions that the data could support.

Assessing the Potential Effects of Public Policies and Investment on Student Achievement

Explaining minority test score gains. Minorities have made significant gains in test scores over the last 20 years and our study shows that a large proportion of these gains was unexplained by family changes. The dramatically rising test scores of minorities have resulted in a significant closing of the achievement gap between minority and nonminority youth and less inequality in educational outcomes. While this is a significant educational accomplishment, a significant gap remains. It is important to understand what factors contributed to these gains and whether they will continue to close the gap in the future.

Hypothesized factors that might explain the residual gains must meet four criteria. First, the hypothesized cause must be either empirically linked to test scores or at least plausibly linked to having an influence on test scores. Second, the factor must have significantly changed for youth who were 14–18 in 1970/1975 versus those who were 14–18 in 1990. Third, it must have affected black and Hispanic scores significantly but had essentially no impact on non-Hispanic white scores. Fourth, it must be a factor that would not be reflected through changing family characteristics.[6]

Changing public policies in the area of equal educational opportunity and increased public investment in children and schools fit these criteria. The policies directed toward providing equal educational opportunity certainly would have been different for 14–18-year-old youth in 1970 who went to school in the late 1950s and 1960s as opposed to similar youth in 1990 who went to school in the late 1970s and 1980s. The barriers that have been removed to equal educational opportunity for blacks primarily involve access to integrated and probably more competitive K–12 schools, and improved access to higher education. While Hispanics might have also been affected by these policies, the policies insuring that language was not a barrier to educational opportunity might also be expected to have an impact on their test scores.

Since the major implementation of these policy changes occurred in the 1970s and 1980s, they would be expected to affect those children growing up and attending school in the time period that corresponds to our sample of 14–18-year-old youth in 1990. The effects of these policy changes would also be expected to primarily affect minority scores but to have little impact on non-Hispanic white scores, and would probably not be reflected through changed family characteristics.

Increases in public investment in K–12 schools and social programs directed at families and children also meet these criteria. There were dramatic increases in real public investment in schools and children from the 1960s through the 1980s. For example, Fuchs and Reklis (1992) estimated that per-capita (real 1988 dollars) public spending

---

[6]To take an example, a suggested candidate for explaining the residual might be decreased viewing of television. If so, one would have to show that students who watch less television score higher, that decreased watching occurred between 1970/1975 and 1990, that the decrease was large for black and Hispanic students but not for non-Hispanic white students, and that the decreased viewing was not simply predicted by higher education level of parents (significant effect in a multivariate model).

on children was $1,289 in 1960 compared to $2,946 in 1988 (about a 3 percent increase per year). Part of this additional spending was specifically targeted toward minority and/or youth from lower-income families. Since a greater proportion of black and Hispanic families have lower incomes, these programs would be expected to differentially affect minority scores.

Although some of the increased spending on K–12 education was not specifically directed toward minority youth, school administrators and teachers may have allocated more resources to lower-scoring youth. Since a greater proportion of black and Hispanic students have lower scores, minority youth would again be expected to be most affected if this occurred. Social programs such as Head Start and child health and nutrition programs directed at children and families also fit this pattern of differential effects for minority youth, although the effect of some of these programs may have been proxied by family variables included in our models.

In addition to public investment and public policies, other possible explanations for minority gains include migration trends that may have placed minorities in different school districts, changing motivation of minority students, and perhaps differential returns to education for minority versus nonminority youth.

One promising area of research is the development of improved statistical models incorporating the effects of multiple risks on children. The child-development and more clinically oriented literature repeatedly focuses on the deleterious effects of multiple-risk factors on children. The hypothesis implies that test scores might fall dramatically (nonlinearly or exponentially) when children are under conditions of multiple risk. Basically, this means that the combined effects on test scores of low family income and low levels of parental education may be much larger than the additive, independent effects of each factor. Some students, then, may experience a slippery slope where achievement falls drastically with every new risk they encounter. But the reverse side of the argument is that for such children, as risks decline, student achievement should go up dramatically as well. The latter, if true, might help explain rapid gains in test scores for lower-achieving children. We are exploring the implications of the multiple-risk hypothesis.

Explaining non-Hispanic white results. The lack of a residual (mathematics) or a small negative residual (verbal/reading) for non-Hispanic whites needs to be explored further. One interpretation is that family effects for nonminorities may be incorrectly captured by a linear model, because marginal differences in income, family size, and parental education affect higher-scoring youth less than lower-scoring youth.[7] If the family effects are smaller in reality, then there would be larger positive residuals for non-Hispanic white youth, who tend to have higher test scores, on average.

A second hypothesis is that the public spending and changed public policies simply did not benefit non-Hispanic whites for several reasons. One is that the most effective policies and programs may have been directed primarily at minorities (desegregation, affirmative action, bilingual programs, etc.). In addition, programs targeted toward all lower-scoring students may have been less effective for non-Hispanic white students because lower-scoring non-Hispanic white students are more often located in rural areas. If rural areas have not received a proportionate share of resources and attention, students there may not have benefited to the same extent as students in urban areas. It may also just be more difficult to help lower-scoring rural youth due to their dispersion and the lack of economies of scale.

A third explanation is that while lower-scoring non-Hispanic white youth benefited from public investment, higher-scoring youth lost ground for several reasons. For instance, some have suggested a weakening of the curriculum for higher-achieving youth (Rock, 1987). Also, there may have been an implicit tradeoff in producing the large gains for minority or lower-scoring youth. Successfully addressing the problems of lower-scoring youth may have resulted in less emphasis and fewer resources for higher-scoring students. These are all important issues that can be explored through future research.

---

[7]We have run fully interactive models with squared terms and used these for estimating family effects. While the more complex models generally make only very small changes (less than 0.02 of a standard deviation) in the estimated size of the family effects, it should be noted that the largest change is for non-Hispanic white students for reading/verbal scores when the results show a decline in family effect of 0.05 of a standard deviation. This reduces the size of the negative residual somewhat for non-Hispanic white students.

The Quality and Productivity of Schools

This study does not support the view that schools of the 1970s and 1980s have deteriorated in significant ways with respect to the schools of the 1950s and 1960s in their instruction in mathematics and verbal/reading skills. Moreover, it suggests that schools have made significant progress in decreasing inequalities between minority and nonminority students. There have been several significant changes in schools in this time period, including school consolidation, large real increases in per-student expenditures, integration of students, changing curriculum, smaller class sizes, and a more experienced and better paid teaching force. Some of these changes may have played a key role in boosting the scores of youth, particularly minority youth.

However, the results are not as positive from the perspective of educational productivity. The concept of educational productivity—similar to that of economic productivity—measures whether learning (output) per unit of resources (input) is rising or falling. Learning can change either because more years of education are achieved or because more learning occurs per year of education. Learning also has a dimension of breadth and depth. Students today may learn a wider array of subjects than students of the past, or they might learn each subject in more depth. There are obvious tradeoffs among the various components of educational productivity. For example, resources can be devoted to keeping youth in school longer, to teaching a broader array of subjects, or to focus more resources on teaching fewer subjects in depth.

While educational productivity has increased with regard to the increased student completion rates over the last 20 years, much less is known about the tradeoff between depth and breadth. For instance, students in the 1950s and 1960s did not spend time learning computer skills, and time tradeoffs may occur between learning new subjects and acquiring less in-depth knowledge of older subjects. Unfortunately, there are no good overall measures of the breadth of student knowledge. Moreover, we do not know the precise level of changing resources devoted to instruction in these areas. It is possible that these added resources were used primarily to add to the breadth of subjects, not their depth.

If we assume a constant level of resources and time devoted to subjects, our analysis suggests that there appear to be no dramatic gains in the educational productivity of schools as measured by the mathematics and verbal/reading test score trends. However, these issues need to be explored further before a full assessment can be made regarding the productivity of schools. Such an assessment would need to take into account changes in curriculum (breadth and depth), time and resources devoted to instruction, and school climate, and how these contribute to educational productivity over time.

FINAL COMMENTS

As discussed above, this study has highlighted several questions that need to be answered through future research. Developing more complex statistical models that more accurately reflect children's development will further clarify the importance of the family, school, and community contexts and their contribution to childhood outcomes. From our discussion, it is clear that we need to be cautious when using averages across all students to gauge changes in test scores. An average tends to obscure the fact that some groups of students may have markedly different results and that conditions for some may have worsened, lowering their achievement scores. Our results should not be interpreted to mean that conditions have improved for every student, family, or school—only that there has been a positive change when averaging across all 14–18-year-old students over the last 20 years.

ACKNOWLEDGMENTS

We are grateful to the Lilly Endowment Inc. for their support of the Institute for Education and Training at RAND, under whose aegis this report was written. We are also grateful to Stephen Sellman, Director of Accession Policy, Office of the Secretary of Defense, for his support and recognition of the commonality of defense and domestic issues with respect to future student achievement. Their support and the support of Georges Vernez and Roger Benjamin, directors of the IET, allowed us to examine these broad and fundamental questions about public policy, the American family, and the educational system.

We are indebted to Paul Hill of RAND and Richard Murnane of Harvard University for their insightful reviews and useful suggestions for improving this report. The report has benefited by comments from Bernard Rostker, director of RAND's Defense Manpower Research Center. We also appreciate the work of Robert Young, who assisted in building the data files, and Luetta Pope and Susan Spindel, who contributed to typing the final document.

Chapter One

INTRODUCTION

PURPOSE OF STUDY

Our current national concern with economic competitiveness and the quality of our schools has focused considerable attention on the subject of student achievement as measured by standardized tests. Test scores are increasingly being used to assess student proficiency and the quality of our education system. Yet test scores themselves are of value only if changes or differences in test scores can be related to factors causing the changes. Then test scores might provide some policy guidance as to what further changes might increase test scores. Unfortunately, there is little agreement about what has caused the changes in national test scores over the last 25 years—and indeed there are even differences in perceptions about what the direction of test scores has been.

Isolating the factors causing changes in test scores is difficult, partly because dramatic changes have occurred in several factors that have been linked to student achievement. These factors include dramatic changes in the characteristics of American families, the demographic characteristics of students in terms of race/ethnicity, and public investment and policies in educational and social programs. Family and demographic characteristics are among the strongest factors explaining differences in test scores. Therefore, the dramatic changes that have taken place in the American family and in demographic trends over the last 20–25 years would be expected to affect trends in student achievement. The changes in the family are often cited as detrimental to children and include an increased proportion of children living in households below the poverty level, in single-parent families, in homes with working mothers, or in families with younger, unwed mothers. The demographic characteristics of the student population have also changed—most dramatically in the proportion of students who are Hispanic. Given these changes, an important question is: Did the family and demographic changes affect student achievement levels over the last 20–25 years?

During this same period, public investment in children and families increased markedly (Fuchs and Reklis, 1992). Per-capita real expenditures in K–12 education more than doubled from 1967 to 1992. In addition, many new programs and policies directed at improving children's outcomes were initiated or expanded. These included Head Start, nutrition and health programs, compensatory education programs, the integration of public schools, and family income support. These programs might also be expected to improve student achievement. However, previous empirical research suggests that their effects might be smaller than those associated with family and demographic changes. As a result, the effect of changing public investment and public policies on test score trends cannot be accurately estimated without first accounting for the changes in the family and demography.

This study develops estimates of the expected effect of changing family and demographic characteristics on student mathematics and reading/verbal test scores of 14–18-year-old students from 1970/1975 and 1990. We develop estimates of family/demographic effects for nationally representative samples of American youth ages 14–15 and 15–18. We also develop separate estimates for Hispanic, black, and non-Hispanic white students. We then compare these estimated changes resulting from families and demographics to actual changes in test scores for nationally representative samples of similarly aged students for similar periods. We use the only national tests that can provide scores for a representative sample of youth over this period—the National Assessment of Educational Progress (NAEP).[1] The difference between actual NAEP changes and estimated effects resulting from family and demographics provides preliminary evi-

---

[1]Chapter Two discusses our reasons for using the NAEP scores rather than Scholastic Aptitude Test (SAT) scores.

dence that factors other than family influence test scores, the most likely candidate being changes in public policy and public investment in education and social programs during the period. Future research is needed to better identify and estimate these effects and their causes.

RELEVANCE TO CURRENT POLICY DEBATES

Many of the current policy debates ongoing in American education are based on differing assumptions about the direction and causes of historical changes in test scores and what these changing test scores imply about the quality of education and the direction of future policies. Although this report cannot address each of these issues described below, further research that builds on this study can inform these debates.

Reliance on Test Scores for Teacher and School Accountability

The perception of declining student achievement and declining school quality despite higher real levels of spending has initiated a movement toward more accountability. Increased testing at the national, state, and local levels is being implemented with an immediate goal of trying to obtain better measures of output and establish a firmer basis for accountability of teachers, schools, and school systems. Underlying this movement is the assumption that simple comparisons of scores over time or between teachers, schools, or school districts can serve as a basis for judging the quality of teaching, schools, or school districts.[2] If changes in family or demographic characteristics underlie changes in test scores, test score comparisons that fail to account for these differences are even more flawed.

---

[2]Koretz (1991) warns against this line of reasoning when he discusses the state NAEP, which he argues "cannot tell us what policies and programs are effective" (pp. 19–20).

Allocating Funds Between Richer and Poorer School Districts

The current debate over allocating state educational expenditures between richer and poorer districts is partly predicated on the assumption that higher test scores in wealthier districts are due to higher expenditures and better school quality. An alternative explanation is that differences in family characteristics account for most or part of these score differences. If so, simple reallocation of school expenditures may not produce better student achievement without also addressing family issues in poorer districts. Without a better understanding of the effect of families compared to schools, these important resource allocation issues between rich and poor districts cannot be answered.

School Reform and School Choice

Part of the motivation for fundamental school reform comes from a common perception that test scores have been stable or have declined over the last 20 years despite the large additional investments made in schools and social programs. This implies that additional investment in education would have little payoff without fundamental reform of the system. However, this hypothesis that additional investments did not have an effect on test scores does not take into account the changes in demographics and the American family and their possible effects on test scores. It is possible that family and demographic changes depressed test scores and the additional public investment prevented even further declines.

One particular reform—school choice—has also been championed by those who point to the higher achievement—and sometimes lower costs—of students in private schools. However, a key question is whether the *private schools* themselves or the characteristics of *families* sending children to private schools are responsible for the higher scores at such schools, and whether the marginal child who transfers to a private school will benefit to the same degree. Again, the relative contribution of families compared to schools is an important underlying issue.

Allocating Public Resources to Schools or Family Support

Another issue is how public investments can most effectively be allocated between expenditures to support education and expenditures to support families. State, local, and federal governments spend about $250 billion annually to support primary and secondary education in the United States. Less than $50 billion is spent on programs aimed at supporting families and children.[3] Whether additional investments in education or additional investments in family programs would provide the larger return on investment is a crucial question, especially given our constrained fiscal environment. Answering this question requires, among other things, better models that provide quantitative estimates of the contributions of family and public investments to student achievement.

Productivity and the Level of School and Family Investment

Our competitive economic position depends partly on the growth of worker productivity and partly on the level of future public resources that will need to be devoted to social spending to pay for programs such as prisons and the criminal justice system, welfare, unemployment, job training programs, and health expenditures arising from treatment of addictions and victims of violent crimes. Both worker productivity and future social spending depend partly on student achievement. Poor achievement in school is frequently associated with dropout behavior and subsequent poor labor-market outcomes (Kaplan and Luck, 1977; Rumberger, 1983; Pallas, 1984; Ekstrom et al., 1986; Wehlage and Rutter, 1986; Wagenaar, 1987; Hagan, 1991; Ensminger and Slusarcick, 1992). Studies of military enlistees have shown that those who score higher on aptitude tests are more likely to perform better on a wide variety of tasks, to more often complete their terms of enlistment, and to have fewer disciplinary problems (Grissmer and Kirby, 1988; Marquis and Kirby, 1989; Kirby and Grissmer, 1993).

A key question is whether higher levels of investment in schools and families would be recouped through better economic performance

---

[3]These expenditures include Aid to Families with Dependent Children (AFDC), various health and nutritional programs, and Head Start.

and reduced future public expenditures. Although there is still much debate concerning the precise link between academic achievement and economic output (Kendrick, 1980; Baily, 1981), a recent article (Bishop, 1989) provides one estimate of the effect of test score declines on productivity growth. Bishop estimates that if test scores had continued to grow at the rate that prevailed between 1942 and 1967, labor quality would have been about 3 percent higher by 1989, and 1987 gross national product (GNP) would have been about $86 billion higher. Indeed, he forecasts that the social cost, in terms of forgone GNP, will double over the next several years and he implies that even if academic achievement rises markedly, the test score decline will continue to depress productivity into the next century. However, a remaining question is: What level of investment would be required to boost test scores? This question may be answered by analyzing the effect of the large additional investments of the last 20 years.

AN OVERVIEW OF METHODOLOGY AND RESULTS

Methodology

Our analysis of the effects of changing family environment and demographic composition on test scores is based on two nationally representative samples of students. The first is the National Longitudinal Survey of Youth (NLSY), which sampled 12,500 14–21-year-old youth in 1979 primarily for the purpose of studying labor-force participation. In 1980, each respondent was given the Armed Services Vocational Aptitude Battery (ASVAB)—a test that measures mathematics, reading, and several other vocational aptitudes. The second is the base year National Education Longitudinal Survey (NELS) of about 25,000 eighth graders in 1988. Mathematics and reading tests were also administered to this sample. Both databases have data on family characteristics collected from both respondents and their parents.

Models relating family characteristics to test scores are developed for 15–18-year-old youth from the NLSY and for eighth graders from the NELS. Using two independently drawn and tested samples for different age groups helps ensure that the results are not specific to a particular age, a particular sample, or a particular test. The set of variables used in the model is limited to variables that are common to both datasets; however, this includes most of the family characteristics that earlier studies have shown to be most strongly related to achievement scores. These are family income, mother's and father's education, mother's age at child's birth, family size, family structure, and the working status of the mother.

The estimated models are then used to predict test scores for the child samples drawn from the 1970, 1975, and 1990 March Current Population Surveys (CPS). These surveys contain a nationally representative sample of U.S. youth and families for those years. This procedure yields predicted test scores for each child, based on family and demographic characteristics at that time. Shifts in the predicted test score distribution over time are due to the interaction of two factors: the importance of the variable in predicting test scores (measured by the estimated coefficient) and the extent of the change in the variable over the relevant time period. We calculate a mean test score for each predicted test score distribution; the difference in the mean test scores provides an estimate of the *net* effects of changing family and demographic characteristics over the time period. We estimate changes for the total population and separately for non-Hispanic white, black, and Hispanic youth.

We compare this difference in mean test scores to actual differences in test scores reported by the NAEP. The NAEP administered tests to nationally representative samples of 9-, 13-, and 17-year-old students from the early 1970s through the 1990s. These comparisons allow us to assess the extent to which family and demographic changes account for actual test score changes and the importance and relevance of other factors in determining test score changes. A gap between actual changes in NAEP scores and our estimates of family and demographic effects provides an initial indicator that other factors may have affected student achievement.

Results

Our results run counter to the "conventional wisdom" that a deteriorating family environment and changing demographics may have lowered test scores. Our results show that the net effects of changes in family and demographic characteristics from 1970 to 1990 would predict higher—not lower—test scores. They show that changing family and demographic characteristics would predict an upward shift in mean verbal and mathematics test scores of between 0.10 and 0.20 of a standard deviation (or 3–7 percentile points) from 1975 to 1990. The results are very similar for children aged 14–15 (the sample to whom the NELS eighth-grade model was fit) and those between 15 and 18 years (the sample to whom the NLSY model was fit). The primary reasons for estimated gains in test scores are significantly higher parental education levels and smaller family size. Our estimates for separate racial/ethnic groups show that the net effect of changing family factors is generally more positive for black and non-Hispanic white children than for Hispanic children.

The NAEP mathematics and reading scores also show gains in test scores for 13- and 17-year-old students that are similar in magnitude to those predicted from family and demographic effects alone. However, there are major differences for demographic groups. The NAEP scores show very large gains for black and Hispanic students but small gains or losses for non-Hispanic white students.

Although we predict significant gains in black test scores because of changing family characteristics, these factors alone can account for only about a third of the substantial gains made by blacks on the NAEP. Similarly, Hispanic students made significant gains on the NAEP that cannot be accounted for by family changes. In contrast, the gains made by non-Hispanic white students on the NAEP can be completely accounted for by family changes. The results imply that there are large residual gains in minority scores not accounted for by family changes, but no residual gains for white students. Perhaps the more viable hypothesis for accounting for these residual gains is increased public investment in schools and social programs and changing social policies such as school desegregation and bilingual education. These factors can plausibly be linked to school achievement, have changed markedly over the last 25 years, and might be expected to affect minority students much more than nonminority students. It is possible that other factors might also account for some of these gains, but it is difficult to think of factors that affect scores, have changed markedly between 1970 and 1990, and would be expected to differentially affect minority students.

ORGANIZATION OF THE REPORT

Chapter Two reviews test score trends and changes in family and demographic composition over the last 20 years, along with previous work attempting to link family and demographic characteristics with test score trends. Chapter Three describes our methodology and data sources. Chapter Four describes the theoretical framework for analyzing family effects on student achievement and several empirical findings from previous literature. Chapter Five presents the results of the multivariate analyses linking family characteristics and achievement scores from both the NLSY and the NELS. Chapter Six tabulates the results of using these equations to predict test scores for national samples of children in 1970, 1975, and 1990. Chapter Seven compares our predictions with the actual NAEP results. Conclusions are presented in Chapter Eight, along with implications and suggestions for future research.

Chapter Two

TEST SCORE TRENDS AND THE CHANGING AMERICAN FAMILY

In this chapter, we first review the trends in national test scores and the trends in family and demographic characteristics. We then review studies that have attempted to relate trends in test scores to changing demographics and family characteristics.

REVIEW OF TRENDS IN NATIONAL TEST SCORES

Only one test has been designed and administered over the last 25 years with the specific purpose of monitoring the average achievement trends of nationally representative samples of American students—the NAEP. We first discuss the trends in these scores, and then discuss the better known SAT and the reasons why the SAT is not a reliable test for monitoring student achievement over time.

The National Assessment of Educational Progress

For more than two decades, the NAEP, funded by the Department of Education, has been the most important source of information on trends in the academic achievement of American students. The NAEP assesses student performance in various subject areas, including reading, mathematics, science, and writing, for nationally representative students at ages 9, 13, and 17. For this study, we used student test score trends in mathematics and reading for 13- and 17-year-old students. The blocks of mathematics and reading questions used to measure trends have been the same since the early 1970s, allowing for accurate trend data.

NAEP develops a nationally representative sample of students through a complex four-stage cross-sectional sample. In the first stage, primary sampling units (PSUs) were derived from dividing the United States into geographic units that consisted of metropolitan statistical areas (MSAs), a single county, or a group of contiguous counties. In the 1990 trend sample, 97 PSUs were selected in the first stage. In the second stage, schools were selected within each PSU with probabilities proportional to assigned measures of size. In the third sample stage, modes of testing were assigned to the schools. In the fourth stage, age-eligible students within schools were randomly selected to take the assessment. Students were not assessed if they had limited English proficiency, were considered mildly mentally retarded (educable), or were functionally disabled (for more details on the NAEP, see Johnson and Allen, 1992).

The NAEP tests were given at approximate four-year intervals in the 1970s and early 1980s and have been given more frequently since then. The earliest tests that can be used as a basis for monitoring trends accurately is the 1971 verbal/reading and the 1973 mathematics test. However, these tests do not identify Hispanic students. The first tests where Hispanic students are identified are the 1975 reading/verbal tests and 1978 mathematics test. Since the proportion of Hispanics has increased markedly, our primary emphasis is on the 1975–1990 verbal and the 1978–1990 mathematics test comparisons.

Figure 2.1 shows the average differences in test scores converted to standard deviation units for 13- and 17-year-old students between 1971 and 1990 for verbal/reading and between 1973 and 1990 for mathematics. For each age group, students scored higher on each test in 1990 than in the earlier period. For 17-year-old students taking the verbal/reading test, a movement of 0.11 of a standard deviation indicates that the average student in 1990 scored about 4 percentile points higher than the corresponding student in 1971. Thus, from the earliest point at which nationally representative samples of students can be tracked using tests with similar test items over time, the evidence shows that students in 1990 did better than students from the early 1970s in both verbal/reading and mathematics scores. However, an important question is whether the gains are different by racial/ethnic groups. This gain in test scores and the differential gains by racial/ethnic groups have been noted earlier by others (e.g., Koretz, 1986, 1992).

RAND*MR488-2.1*

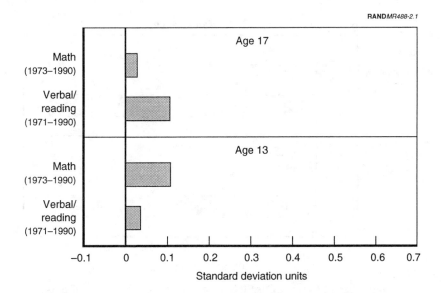

Figure 2.1—Change in NAEP Scores by Age and Type of Test

Figures 2.2 and 2.3 show changes in mathematics and verbal/reading scores for black and nonblack students for similar periods. The data show that both 13- and 17-year-old black students have made very substantial gains—between 0.55 and 0.7 of a standard deviation—in both mathematics and verbal/reading scores between the early 1970s and 1990. The scores of the nonblack population have either gained or lost about 0.1 of a standard deviation. The large gains in black scores have almost cut in half the gap in black/nonblack test scores that existed in the early 1970s.

Part of the reason for small gains or losses for nonblacks could be the large increase in Hispanic students, so it is also important to separate the scores of the black, Hispanic, and non-Hispanic white student population. The first time that Hispanic students were identified separately in the NAEP tests was in the verbal/reading tests given in 1975 and the mathematics tests given in 1978. Figures 2.4 and 2.5 show the changes in mathematics and verbal/reading scores of the black, Hispanic, and non-Hispanic white population for these tests. The score differences show that black students made the largest

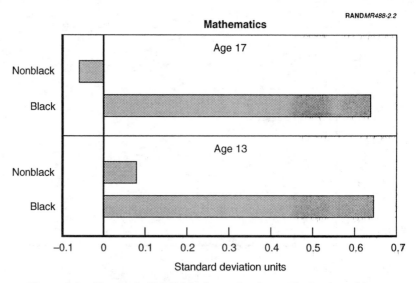

Figure 2.2—Change in NAEP Mathematics Scores by Race and Age
Group Between 1973 and 1990

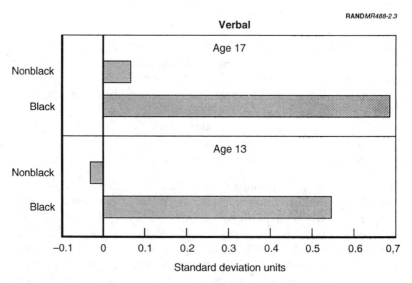

Figure 2.3—Change in NAEP Verbal Scores by Race and Age Group
Between 1971 and 1990

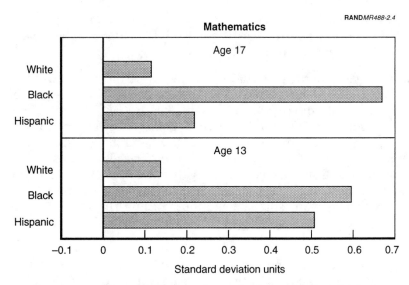

Figure 2.4—Change in NAEP Mathematics Scores by Racial/Ethnic and Age Group Between 1978 and 1990

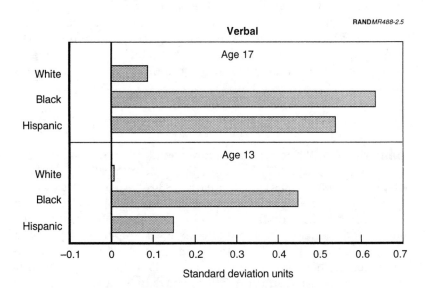

Figure 2.5—Change in NAEP Verbal Scores by Racial/Ethnic and Age Group Between 1975 and 1990

gains in these time periods but that Hispanic students also made significant gains, with non-Hispanic white students either making small gains or showing losses.

The larger minority gains have partially closed the gap between minority and nonminority scores. Figures 2.6 and 2.7 show the gaps between racial/ethnic groups in mathematics and verbal/reading scores for the 1975–1990 time period. For both age groups and both tests, the gains made by blacks have decreased the test score differences by approximately 40 percent. There has also been a smaller, but still significant reduction in the gap between non-Hispanic white and Hispanic scores. A gap still exists in 1990 between the scores of black and Hispanic students and those of non-Hispanic white students, but the size of that gap has been significantly reduced since the 1970s.

These results, showing gains in scores from the 1970s to 1990 for each age group and test, with sizable gains for minority groups, often run counter to the public perception of the direction and pattern of student achievement. Public opinion about declines in student achievement and the quality of schools is partly based on trends in the SAT, which show declines in mathematics and verbal scores. SAT scores are highly influential in shaping public opinion. Unfortunately, there are problems in using the SAT to gauge trends in test scores or make judgments about the quality of American education.

Scholastic Aptitude Tests

Comparing NAEP and SAT test score trends. The trends in the SAT are shown in Figure 2.8. The average test score declined markedly between the late 1960s and the early 1980s. Mean scores on the mathematics portion declined 26 points from 1967 to 1981. The decline was even larger on the verbal portion: 42 points over the same time period. Since then, the mathematics scores have risen somewhat and leveled off, but they are still 16 points below the 1967 levels. Verbal scores increased slightly during 1985–1987 but appear to be on a downward trend and currently are back to the low score of 1981.

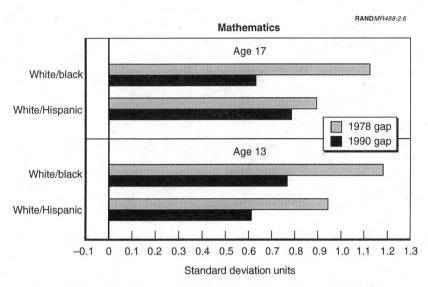

Figure 2.6—Gap in NAEP Mathematics Scores by Racial/Ethnic
Group in 1978 and 1990

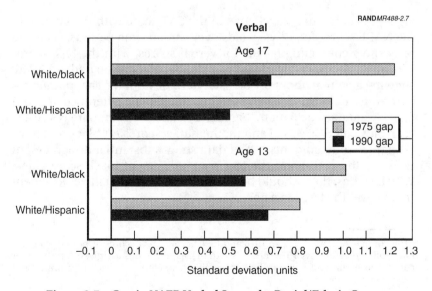

Figure 2.7—Gap in NAEP Verbal Scores by Racial/Ethnic Group
in 1975 and 1990

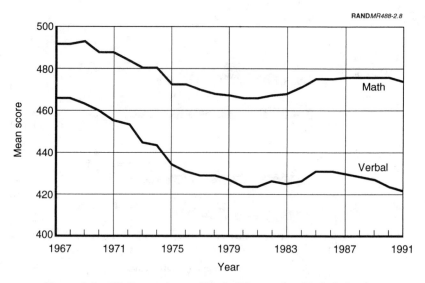

Figure 2.8—Mathematics and Verbal Scores for the Scholastic Aptitude Test, 1967–1991

Figure 2.9 compares the change in the SAT score with the change in the NAEP scores for 17-year-olds over similar time periods. The two tests show conflicting results for verbal scores, with the SAT scores showing a decline of nearly 0.3 of a standard deviation and the NAEP showing a gain of about 0.1 of a standard deviation. The mathematics trends are in closer agreement but still show a difference of about 0.1 of a standard deviation. Figures 2.10 and 2.11 compare NAEP 17-year-olds and SAT verbal and mathematics scores for black and non-Hispanic white students.[1] The data show substantial disagreement between the NAEP and the SAT over the size of black score gains. Which scores, then, should be used for tracking student achievement trends over the last 25 years?

---

[1]The comparisons are between 1976 and 1990 because SAT scores by ethnic group are not available before the 1976 test. Also, the Hispanic scores are given separately by country of origin and may not be comparable over time, so Hispanic comparisons have been excluded.

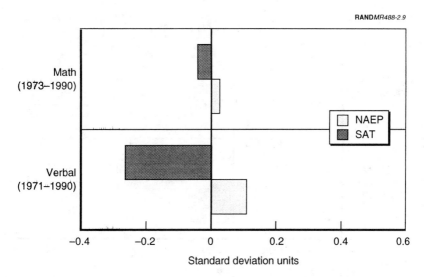

Figure 2.9—Changes in SAT and NAEP Scores

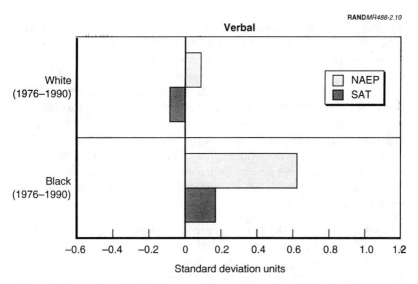

Figure 2.10—Changes in NAEP and SAT Verbal Scores by Race

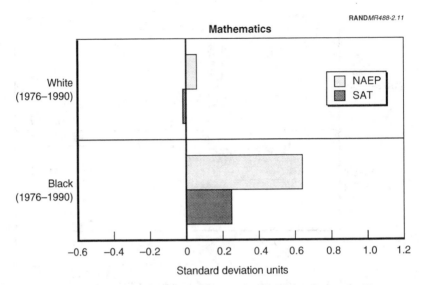

Figure 2.11—Changes in NAEP and SAT Mathematics Scores by Race

Analyses of a wider set of test score measures that have more statistically reliable samples than the SAT leave little doubt that test scores of representative samples of American youth probably declined during the 1960s and somewhat into the 1970s but overall have not declined and probably have increased over the last 20 years (Koretz, 1986, 1987, 1992; Linn and Dunbar, 1990). In addition to the NAEP tests of 9-, 13-, and 17-year-old students, the Iowa Tests of Basic Skills and the norming tests for the Preliminary Scholastic Aptitude Tests show higher scores (Linn and Dunbar, 1990). This latter test is administered by the College Board to a nationally drawn sample at approximate six-year intervals, and the results show no evidence of declining test scores.

Problems with the SAT tests for monitoring trends. The SAT trends are misleading as indicators of achievement trends for American youth for two reasons. The first is that the sample of youth taking the test is not selected by the College Board to represent any particular sample of U.S. youth. Rather, the SAT sample is self-selected, meaning that whoever applies to take the SAT test determines the sample for that year. As a result, each year the sample changes in size and composition. The size and composition have changed markedly over time and primarily reflect the increasing proportion of seniors wanting to apply and enter college. In general, the effect of changing sample size and composition has been a downward bias in test score trends. However, the size of this selection bias cannot be accurately estimated, since the College Board does not collect several important control variables that could be used to estimate year-to-year corrections.

The shifting size and composition of the SAT population is significant. In 1967 about 30 percent of high school seniors took the test; by 1992, this proportion had increased to 40 percent. Researchers believe that this increasing proportion may account for part of the decline in test scores during the late 1960s and early 1970s, since the additional students taking the tests generally have come from a lower achieving population (Rock, 1987). However, the effect of changing size since the early 1970s is more uncertain.

In addition to changing sample size, the composition of the test population has changed, with increasing proportions being minorities and women. Minorities—on average—score lower on achievement tests; women have significantly different patterns in verbal and mathematics scores than men. Changes in year-to-year SAT scores can reflect changing sample size and changing sample composition, as well as real changes in student achievement, and it is not possible to separate these effects. Thus, changes in SAT scores should not be used to measure achievement trends.

Although the bias in the SAT resulting from self-selection has been the most publicized and studied, the SAT scores are subject to an even more potentially serious bias. The SAT is taken by only about 40 percent of high school seniors—those who plan on applying to college. Since other tests have shown that the primary gains in achievement over the last 20 years have probably occurred among lower-scoring and minority students (Linn and Dunbar, 1990; Johnson and Allen, 1992), *the SAT probably misses those students who have registered the largest score gains.* The combined effect of self-selection and failure to include these lower-scoring students—both of which downwardly bias the SAT scores—makes the SAT trends highly misleading indicators of trends in achievement among American students.

SAT scores and public opinion. Despite convincing analytical evidence of the SAT's inherent downward bias, public opinion continues to rely on the SAT scores. However, this may not be as puzzling as it first appears. Theories regarding how people make inferences concerning statistical data help explain why an impression of declining test scores might develop and persist. For example, Nisbett and Ross (1980) review evidence showing that people make inferential judgments from data that are more salient, vivid, emotionally interesting, and frequently reported than from data that are more statistically accurate but not as widely reported.

Since the SAT tests have been taken by one-third to one-half of American students annually for over 30 years and the results are quite critical to the college admissions process, these tests have much greater exposure and leave vivid impressions on students and parents alike. They are often reported several times a year in different forms—national results, state results, and school district and school results. In addition, local school scores are often used as a basis for judging school quality, desirability, and even real estate values.

In contrast, the NAEP tests, which provide a more statistically accurate picture of test score trends, are taken approximately every four years by small samples of American students and have virtually no effect on the lives of individual students who take them. Thus, it is not surprising that people tend to give more weight to the SAT results than to the NAEP scores.

Research also indicates that mixed evidence—for example, evidence that NAEP scores are moving in an opposite direction from that of the SAT scores—often results in stronger, not weaker, trust in the originally held belief (Nisbett and Ross, 1980). This is partly because people tend to select and read information that agrees with prior expectations. As such, the more frequently reported SAT will tend to reinforce people's beliefs, whereas the less frequently reported NAEP scores might easily be dismissed. In addition, the understanding required to make judgments about the statistical validity of samples is not widespread. Thus, despite their superior sampling procedures, the NAEP or similar tests simply will not be used by most people to make judgments concerning test score trends as long as SAT scores are available.

The potential damage from public opinions based on SAT performance is exacerbated if individuals believe that lower scores reflect the declining quality of schools. Nisbett and Ross (1980) also suggest that such naive inferences are consistent with evidence about how people form such inferences. In particular, people have strong tendencies toward "single cause" explanations and tend to choose those that resemble the effect. Thus, the commonly held association between schools and test scores would lead to naive judgments such as declining test scores being the result of declining school quality. Actually, studies of achievement repeatedly show that family and demographic characteristics have stronger effects on scores than differences in schools or teachers (Coleman et al., 1966; Coleman and Hoffer, 1987; Jencks et al., 1972; Gamoran, 1987). Variables measuring school, teacher, or community characteristics are nearly always far weaker and more inconsistent in explaining the variance in test scores than are demographic or family factors. Unfortunately, the SAT tests do not collect essential family characteristics needed to account for their effects. Since they cannot account for changing demographic and family characteristics, changes in SAT scores can provide no sound evidence concerning the quality of American education.

Although the SAT test might provide useful information concerning an individual student's college performance, any reporting of aggregated unadjusted scores across schools, districts, states, or the nation not only appears to serve no useful public purpose but contributes to misleading impressions about schools and students. Terminating the publication of unadjusted aggregated SAT scores would remove these misleading data that are so influential in shaping public opinion. It might also lead to quicker funding and initiation of the collection of more valid, policy-relevant data.

THE CHANGING AMERICAN FAMILY

Given the increase in test scores among nationally representative samples of youth over the last 20 years, we need to examine whether the "deteriorating" family environment and changing demographics may actually have prevented even further gains. We now review that issue.

Increasing test scores occurred during a period of dramatic changes in the structure of families and in demography. Many sociodemographic trends mentioned in the literature and popular press are viewed as having adverse effects on family environment and educational outcomes (Zill and Rogers, 1988; Fuchs and Reklis, 1992; Zill, 1992). Among the more prominent trends mentioned are:

- A soaring divorce rate that has resulted in a higher incidence of single-parent families, primarily headed by single women. By 1986, the number of children under the age of 18 who were living with their mothers only was 13.2 million, an increase of 76 percent over the number of such children in 1970. Although the effects of divorce upon children are debated, Uhlenberg and Eggebeen (1986) point to three particularly detrimental consequences of divorce to the overall well-being of the child: emotional upheaval associated with the divorce, decline in family income, and the sharp decline in the time spent with the noncustodial parent. Survey data reveal that only one in six children living with their mothers had weekly contact with their fathers after the divorce. However, divorce can also remove a child from a conflictual family environment—a condition that has been shown to be detrimental to a child.

- A sharp rise in the birth rate of single mothers, particularly among minorities. For example, in 1970, 10.7 percent of all births were to unmarried women; by 1985, this had climbed to 22.0 percent. About 60 percent of all black births and 28 percent of Hispanic births were to unmarried mothers, compared to less than 15 percent of births to white mothers. In fact, in 1988, about 42 percent of all first births in the United States were to a mother who was either unmarried, a high school dropout, or a teenager; 11 percent were at risk for all three conditions (Zill, 1992). There is some reason to believe that the adolescent pregnancy rate underestimates the rise in pregnancies among unmarried adolescents, because of the sharp rise in the abortion rate among this group. In addition, there are other consequences of sexual behavior that also create additional problems for teenagers—for example, the number of adolescents contracting venereal diseases has grown rapidly (Uhlenberg and Eggebeen, 1986).

- An increase in the number of children living in poverty, after a sharp decline during the late 1960s and early 1970s. In 1986, 20 percent of children under age 18 were below the poverty line; for black and Hispanic children, these rates were 43 and 37 percent, respectively. One reason for this high poverty rate is the high incidence of single-parent families, generally female-headed households, which tend to have far lower incomes than those of two-parent families. Poverty brings with it a whole range of risks: poor adolescents are 50 percent more likely to have physical or mental disabilities; poor young adults, regardless of race or ethnic background, are three times more likely to drop out of high school; low-income teenagers are more likely to be victims of violence (Simons, Finlay, and Yang, 1991).

- A marked increase in the civilian labor-force participation rate of women with children under the age of 18. As of 1990, 68 percent of married women with children under the age of six were working part-time or full-time outside of the home, compared to about 30 percent in 1970. This growth in maternal labor-force participation is popularly cited as a negative influence on the well-being of children.

Uhlenberg and Eggebeen (1986) elaborate on this point and its relationship to the well-being of children:

> And as mothers increasingly work outside of the home, the interaction between mother and child, as well as parental supervision, inevitably declines . . . . From the perspective of the child, it appears that parents are becoming available at times convenient to the parents, not at times when the child has the most need for attention [p. 37].

All of these factors have led to the general perception that the family environment in which children are being nurtured has deteriorated over the last 20 years. Perhaps, Fuchs and Reklis (1992) capture the current mood best:

> American children are in trouble. Not all children, to be sure, but many observers consider today's children to be worse off than their parents' generations in several important dimensions of physical, mental, and emotional well-being [p. 41].

In addition to these factors, there has been a dramatic demographic shift in the racial/ethnic composition of families. Over the time period, 1975–1990, the proportion of Hispanic children in the population increased sharply from 5.8 percent in 1975 to 9.5 percent in 1990—an increase of over 60 percent; the proportion of black teens increased very slightly over the same time period, from 13.5 percent to 13.9 percent. Minority students tend to score lower on standardized tests than nonminority students and the increasing proportion of minority students would tend to lower average test scores.

LINKING CHANGING FAMILY CHARACTERISTICS AND TEST SCORE TRENDS

Several studies have suggested a link between changing family and demographic characteristics and trends in test scores (Koretz, 1987, 1992; Fuchs and Reklis, 1992; Armor, 1992). Koretz (1987) mentions four family- and demographic-related variables in his list of potential factors affecting the trends in test scores: family size/birth order, single-parent households, maternal employment, and ethnic composition. The report concludes that family size/birth order and ethnic composition could have made very modest contributions to trends in scores, but that the evidence for contributions from increases in single-parent families and maternal employment were inconsequential or inconsistent.

Fuchs and Reklis (1992) do not make explicit connections between family characteristics and test scores, but they cite several trends in family characteristics between 1960 and 1988 and suggest that lower test scores are one possible outcome of these trends. These adverse trends include increasing numbers of children living in poverty, a rise in the birth rate of unwed mothers, and increases in the numbers of single-parent families and working mothers. However, they also are the first to emphasize the three *positive* trends in children's environment during this period—an increase in the parental education level, an increase in the income per child, and a significant increase in real governmental spending directed at youth. The latter figure includes elementary and secondary school spending as well as all programs directed at the health and welfare of children. Income per child has increased although family income has been fairly stable because the number of children per family has declined markedly.

Armor (1992) analyzes factors that might account for the large gains in black students' test scores over the last 20 years. He considers three factors: desegregation, compensatory programs, and socioeconomic changes. He concludes that the rising education level of black parents is probably the most important component for explaining black test score gains. For instance, he estimates that about 8 of the 19 point gain on NAEP scores might be accounted for by rising parental education levels. He states:

> The strongest correlate of black achievement gains in the NAEP appears to be improvements in the socioeconomic status of black families, the size of which is comparable to the gains in achievement. This explanation is consistent with the large body of educational research that identifies socioeconomic status as the strongest influence on both black and white achievement [p. 80].

SUMMARY

We reviewed the trends in national tests and discussed their strengths and weaknesses. We pointed out that public opinion is sharply influenced by the SAT; however, the SAT is not a valid indicator of the average achievement of American students. Rather, the NAEP, which repeatedly assesses student achievement using representative samples, is a much better source of data on achievement trends. Thus, we rely on the NAEP trends in our analysis.

This chapter also reviewed studies that attempt to link test score trends to family/demographic characteristics. None of these studies, however, attempted to directly quantify the *net* effects of demographics and important family factors using national samples of youth. They generally relied solely on whether family factors considered one at a time show trends similar to those shown by the test scores. However, univariate relationships can be somewhat misleading when more than one factor is important in explaining test scores and when some factors do not overtly mimic the changes in test scores. This study uses a multivariate model linking test scores, demographics, and family characteristics that allows us to make quantitative estimates of the *net* effect of changing demographics and several changing family characteristics on test score trends. We use these equations to actually predict and compare test scores in

1970 and 1990. Although our work significantly extends previous research, it represents a first step in model building and some uncertainty still remains regarding the precise effects of different characteristics on test scores. Further research is currently under way—this includes extending and refining the present model to take into account interactions and nonlinearities in relationships, and using the unique strengths of each database separately rather than restricting the models to variables common to the two datasets.

The next chapter presents our data and methodology.

Chapter Three

METHODOLOGY AND DATA

METHODOLOGY

This study develops estimates of the net effect of the changing family and demographic environment on student verbal/reading and mathematics test scores over time, and an estimate of the effect of factors not associated with family and demographic changes. The methodology consists of three steps: (1) developing equations relating student achievement to family and demographic characteristics; (2) using these equations to predict test scores for each student in a national sample in 1970, 1975, and 1990 using their family and demographic characteristics; and (3) comparing the mean differences in these predicted test scores (estimates of the effect of changing family and demographic characteristics) to actual scores from the NAEP. This procedure provides an estimate of how much family and demographic changes contributed to actual changes in test scores, and the residual changes in test scores (actual minus family and demographic effect) provide an estimate of the effect that other factors had on changing test scores. The methodology is illustrated in Figure 3.1.

Modeling Student Achievement

Figure 3.2 illustrates schematically the first step of our methodology.

We first estimate models linking test scores to family and demographic characteristics using two quite different nationally representative samples of adolescents. Both samples were given mathematics

RAND *MR488-3.1*

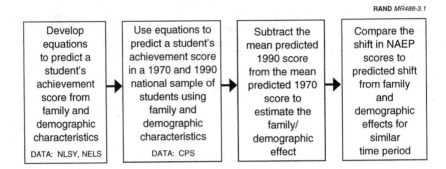

Figure 3.1—Illustration of Methodology

RAND *MR488-3.2*

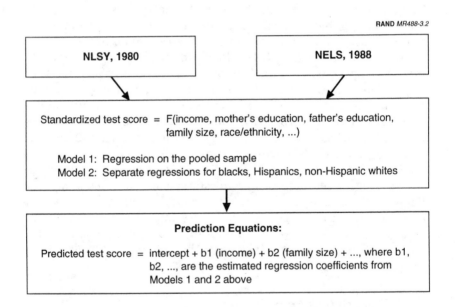

Figure 3.2—Step 1: Modeling Student Achievement

and verbal/reading achievement tests and data were collected on family characteristics. The samples are for different age groups, use different stratification criteria, and use different achievement tests.

We use both sets to make independent estimates of the family and demographic effects to see if the results are sensitive to a particular age group, sample size, sample stratification, or achievement test. However, because we specify similar models across both datasets, we were restricted to choosing measures of family and demographic characteristics that were common to both. Fortunately, the datasets included the most important family and demographic variables that have been shown to be related to achievement.

The datasets are the NLSY, 1980, from which we selected students aged 15–18 years, and the NELS, 1988, which samples eighth graders. The dependent variable in the models is the standardized test score for mathematics and verbal/reading tests and it is assumed to be a function of a set of independent family and demographic variables that are common to both surveys. These include family income, family structure (single mother or two-parent households), family size, parental education, labor-force participation of the mother, and age of the mother at child's birth.

For both the NLSY and the NELS samples, we estimate models relating family characteristics to test scores for the full sample (i.e., pooling all racial/ethnic groups) and for separate population groups— blacks, Hispanics, and non-Hispanic whites. The models described in the body of the report are based on the unweighted samples, although weighted regressions were also estimated and are reported in Appendix C. We note differences in the magnitude of some of the coefficients estimated from the weighted and unweighted regressions in Chapter Five. However, there is little difference in the predicted test scores from the two models (Step 2 of the methodology).

Predicting Test Scores for Samples of Youth

The second step in our methodology is illustrated in Figure 3.3, which shows that the prediction equations derived from estimating Models 1 and 2 are used to predict test scores at the individual level for a representative sample of U.S. children of similar ages in 1970, 1975, and 1990, using family and child characteristics extracted from

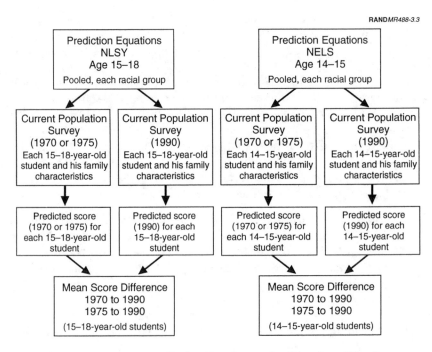

Figure 3.3—Step 2: Predicting Test Scores for Samples of Youth

the March Current Population Surveys. For the 1970 and 1990 comparison, we make predictions using two racial/ethnic groups: black and nonblack.[1] This procedure yields a distribution of predicted test scores for 1970 and 1990. Changes in this test score distribution will reflect both the relative strength of individual family and demographic factors on test scores (as captured by the estimated coefficients in the equations) and the extent to which each factor changed over the time period. We then compute the difference in the mean values of the distribution of test scores for 1970 and 1990 to provide an overall measure of the net effect of changing family characteristics on test scores.

---

[1]We limit ourselves to black/nonblack comparisons for the 1970–1990 period because the CPS does not identify Hispanics in 1970.

We also estimate family and demographic effects from 1975 to 1990 using three racial/ethnic groups: non-Hispanic whites, Hispanics, and blacks.

Comparing Differences in Mean Predicted Test Scores to Actual Scores from the NAEP

The third step (shown in Figure 3.4) is to compare the changes in test scores predicted from changes in family and demographic characteristics from these nationally representative samples to actual changes in test scores from the NAEP. We compare the NLSY results for 15–18-year-old youth to NAEP scores for 17-year-olds, and the NELS results for eighth graders to NAEP results for 13-year-olds.

DATA

National Longitudinal Survey of Youth

The NLSY is a longitudinal survey of 12,686 civilian and military youth aged 14–21 starting in 1979 (Center for Human Resource

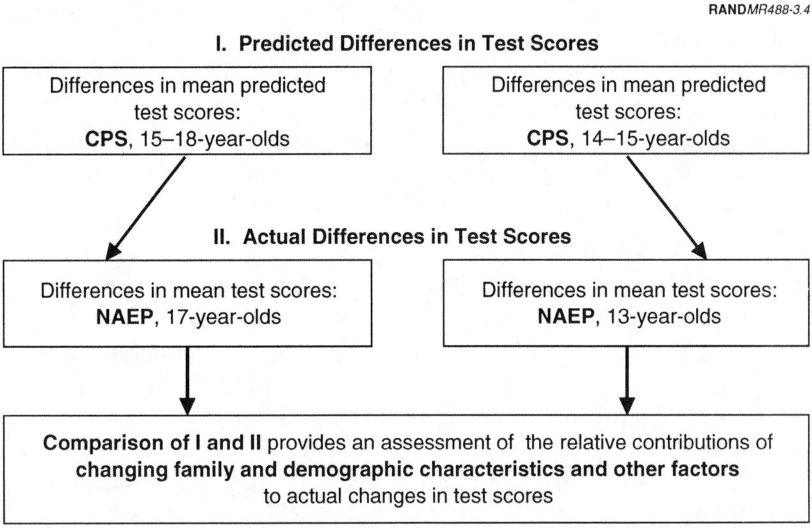

RAND*MR488-3.4*

I. Predicted Differences in Test Scores

Differences in mean predicted test scores:
CPS, 15–18-year-olds

Differences in mean predicted test scores:
CPS, 14–15-year-olds

II. Actual Differences in Test Scores

Differences in mean test scores:
NAEP, 17-year-olds

Differences in mean test scores:
NAEP, 13-year-olds

Comparison of I and II provides an assessment of the relative contributions of **changing family and demographic characteristics and other factors** to actual changes in test scores

Figure 3.4—Step 3: Predicted Differences in Test Scores with Changes in NAEP Test Scores

Research, 1992). It consists of three distinct subsamples: (1) a cross-section sample designed to be representative of noninstitutionalized civilian youth residing in the United States in 1979 and born between 1957 and 1964; (2) a supplemental sample that oversamples civilian Hispanic, black, and economically disadvantaged non-Hispanic, nonblack youth; and (3) a military sample of youth born between 1957 and 1961 and serving in the military as of September 30, 1978. All civilian sample selection was done through a multistage stratified area probability sample of dwelling units and group quarters, with a moderate degree of oversampling to obtain sufficient samples of the targeted groups in the supplemental sample. The sample has been followed from 1979 and surveyed each year, although the military sample was dropped as of 1985, and the supplemental sample was last interviewed in 1990. Of the 12,686 who constituted the original sample in 1979, about 96 percent or 12,141 were retained in the sample for the 1980 survey round.

In 1980, the Department of Defense used the NLSY sample to update the norms of the ASVAB, a multidimensional achievement test, consisting of 10 subtests (Bock and Moore, 1984). A total of 11,914 civilian and military NLSY respondents completed the test. The test is generally regarded as a reasonable proxy for what might be considered general intellectual achievement or GIA. This is a summary term for the developed cognitive abilities, competencies, and knowledge that contribute to productivity in most jobs. It has also been shown that trends of aptitude tests scores (such as the ASVAB) parallel trends for achievement tests (Koretz, 1986) and correlate well with broad spectrum achievement tests (Bishop, 1989).

Our analysis sample is restricted to 15–18-year-olds in 1980 and only the civilian sample (both the cross-section and the low-income sample) for two reasons. First, family income data were collected for the household in which the individual resides; for young people aged 19–22 and those in the military, this household was often a separate household established by the individual, and the income data do not match the "family" income data for younger respondents. Second, this group is more homogeneous in terms of major activities and experience. Most of the 15–18-year-olds are still in school, whereas the 19–22-year-old age group includes college students and employed (for example, those in the military) and unemployed labor-force participants.

For each respondent in the selected sample, we computed an average mathematics score by taking a simple average of the individual raw scores on the arithmetic reasoning and numerical operations subtests; for the verbal score, we used an average of the raw scores on the word knowledge and paragraph comprehension subtests.[2]

National Educational Longitudinal Survey of 1988

The 1988 NELS surveyed and tested about 25,000 eighth-grade students in 1,035 American schools during the base year 1988.[3] Sponsored by the National Center for Education Statistics (NCES), this survey was a two-stage, stratified probability sample with schools selected as the first-stage unit and students within schools as the second-stage unit (for more details see Ingels et al., 1990). After random selection of schools, 26 eighth graders within each school were randomly selected; if schools had fewer than 26 students, all eligible students were included. Some schools were oversampled to ensure that adequate numbers of students were available from sub-populations of interest (e.g., Hispanic/Latinos and Asians).

In addition to these student data, parents were surveyed about family characteristics, their educational expectations for their child, their involvement in school activities, and financial support for future schooling. Parent data were available for about 94 percent of the students in the base year. The survey requested that the parent who was better informed about the child's learning activities fill out the questionnaire. Of the parent survey respondents, about 80 percent were mothers, 17 percent were fathers, and the remaining 3 percent were other male or female guardians. For the purposes of this study, measures of family characteristics were based on parent reports rather than student information because parents are more likely to

---

[2]We did not specifically adjust the test scores to account for the fact that individuals were of different ages when they took the test in 1980. Older students did better, in general, on the ASVAB than younger students. However, we tested versions of the NLSY models with specific age dummies and found that only the intercept term was affected. The intercept term reported in Chapter Five is thus a weighted average of the test scores for 15–18-year-olds.

[3]There are both public and restricted-use versions of the NELS data; we analyzed the restricted-use data files.

offer valid information about family income, parental education, and other sensitive family aspects (see Kaufman and Rasinski, 1991).

NELS contains student test scores in the areas of mathematics, reading, science, and history/government (see Rock and Pollack, 1991). Only the mathematics and reading tests were analyzed for this report. The reading test consisted of 21 multiple-choice items that measured student comprehension and interpretation of five short passages that varied in length from one paragraph to a half-page. The eighth graders were given 21 minutes to complete this test. The mathematics test lasted longer, 30 minutes; it contained 40 items and required students to make quantitative comparisons and to provide answers to word problems, diagrams, and calculations.

March Current Population Surveys

We used the March CPS to obtain nationally representative samples of families of 15–18-year-olds and 14–15-year-olds for 1970, 1975, and 1990. The monthly CPS is the primary data source for obtaining labor-force statistics on employment and wages of U.S. civilian households. An expanded version of the monthly CPS is given in March to a much larger, representative sample of the civilian U.S. population. The data collected include an extensive set of information on each household from which several family characteristics can be derived, including family income, family size, age and education of mother and father, working status of mother, and whether single- or two-parent households. The prediction sample sizes for the 14–15-year-olds ranged between 5,000 and 6,000, somewhat smaller (4,200) for 1990; for the 15–18-year-olds, the sample sizes were between 10,000 and 12,000 (again somewhat smaller for 1990— 8,000). Only those children living with parents or adults were included in the prediction samples.

SUMMARY

This chapter presents the various steps used to estimate family/demographic effects on student achievement trends and describes the databases analyzed in the study. To reiterate, these steps include: (1) estimating the effects of family and demographic characteristics on student achievement using NLSY and NELS; (2) predicting test scores for youth in the 1970, 1975, and 1990 CPS using our models in step (1); and (3) comparing the mean differences estimated from the CPS to the actual differences in the NAEP. This allows us to measure how much family and demographic changes contributed to actual changes in test scores. The residual changes in test scores suggest that other factors affected changes in test scores besides the family and demographic characteristics included in our models.

Chapter Four

STUDENT ACHIEVEMENT AND FAMILY CHARACTERISTICS: LITERATURE REVIEW

NEED FOR A MORE COMPREHENSIVE FRAMEWORK

Developing a theoretical framework that links student achievement and family and demographic characteristics is a critical part of developing improved hypotheses and models. Such a review would need to draw from several disciplinary and interdisciplinary areas of study. These would include literature from traditional educational research, sociology, economics, child development, child psychopathology, clinical psychology, and family systems theory. Each area has developed strands of a theory and has a developed literature that could be used to formulate hypotheses and better understand the complex relationships between families and student achievement. To illustrate, we briefly review three disciplinary views of families and schools from economics, child development, and sociology.

THREE PERSPECTIVES ON THE FAMILY AND STUDENT ACHIEVEMENT

Each perspective starts with a different paradigm or framework concerning what is important in producing youth outcomes, and each uses methods and approaches tailored to their field of study.

The basic economic model linking child achievement to family characteristics has as its foundation both theories of production as well as the human capital approach explicated by Becker (1981) and Becker and Tomes (1986). Parents are assumed to help their children achieve, using parental time, family resources, and the child's innate endowment as inputs. Thus, although there is some transmission of genetic ability, a child's achievement is also conditioned on the learning environment that parents provide and on their preferences for schooling and achievement. This model specifies achievement as a function of parental income, parental time, parental tastes for learning, and the ability endowment of the child, inherited from the parents. There is assumed an inherent tradeoff between child "quantity and quality." That is, the more children in a family—other things equal—the fewer the resources that will be available per child. Intrafamily allocation of resources toward activities that develop achievement as well as different allocations to different children help explain differences in children's outcomes. An overall budget constraint is imposed by family income and market prices, including the opportunity cost of parental time.

This resource-oriented model helps explain why family income levels, family size, and parental education levels might be important in explaining differences in test scores. Effects of working mothers and single-parent families—other things equal—are also seen from a resource perspective—less time available from parents for children. It has a harder time explaining why children of younger parents—other things equal—might score lower. A primary problem with this perspective is it deals only with resources of time and money, and takes no account of the emotional resources necessary for a child's development as well as differences in parenting skills.

The developmental perspective that spans areas of study including child psychology, child development and psychopathology, and family systems theory is anchored more in the study of emotional resources within the family and their effect on individual children's development. Children are assumed to be quite different in the timing and direction of their development, and to be sensitive to different environments. Intellectual development is seen as a gradual unfolding in stages, in keeping with the increased internal ability of the child to handle more complex phenomena. Success at later stages of development depends on successful learning of tasks at earlier stages. Emphasis is placed on the role of parents in establishing emotional bonds to the child, and providing appropriate continuing emotional support as well as a structured and stable environment conducive to learning.

Many family environments are identified as being detrimental to the development of the child and eventual achievement (these are often referred to as dysfunctional families). Such families are characterized by parental conflict, character or psychiatric disorders in parents (depression, schizophrenia, etc.), and emotional, physical, or sexual abuse of children. Literature on this topic also points to several health conditions that can lead to differences in achievement such as hyperactivity, attention deficit disorder, lead poisoning, and depression. A particular hypothesis that arises from clinical work in this field is the multiple-risk hypothesis, which posits that children can be resilient to some adverse conditions, but they face serious achievement failures when they are subjected to several.

Developmental theory has a very richly conceived theory of children's developmental path, but it often ignores the larger resource-allocation questions that inevitably arise when scarce public resources need to be allocated across large groups of children. In this area, a melding together of economic and developmental theories could offer richer insights.

A strand of sociological theory views schools as playing a primary role in increasing student achievement, and this research focuses on determining the characteristics of schools (per-pupil expenditures, organization, class sizes, environment, tracking modes, etc.), teachers, curriculum, and textbooks that can explain variances in test scores. In this literature, family variables are acknowledged as explaining part of the variance and are included usually as control variables so that the school-related variables of interest can be measured accurately. However, there has generally been little emphasis on explaining why family characteristics are related to test scores (Coleman and Hoffer, 1987).

More recent literature in this field acknowledges the role of parents in helping schools in their teaching roles. This literature emphasizes cultural differences among families of different origins as helping explain achievement score differences. Differences in parenting styles have also been identified as determinants of student achievement. However, the emphasis still remains on making schools more effective as the primary option to boosting student achievement.

As part of the broader study, we are developing an integrated framework that draws on these various perspectives (as well as others). However, extant data for examining factors affecting student achievement over time do not have the necessary information to capture the complexities suggested by this interdisciplinary framework. Given that our primary purpose here is to examine the extent to which changes in family and demographic characteristics accounted for test score trends, we have restricted our analyses to the set of variables that is common to several national databases.

The next subsection discusses the findings from previous studies that examine the link between family and demographic characteristics and student achievement within multivariate models.

EMPIRICAL LITERATURE: FAMILY CHARACTERISTICS AND STUDENT ACHIEVEMENT

Our selection of variables in our analytical models was dictated by two considerations: (a) comparability across the datasets used for estimation purposes (NLSY and NELS); and, (b) availability of the same variables on the datasets used for prediction (March CPS files). Rather than attempt an exhaustive summary of the literature on student achievement and its determinants, we focus our attention on findings that relate to the family variables that are included in our models.

Family Structure

As we had seen earlier, it has frequently been argued that children in single-parent households may be shortchanged in terms of both money and time and thus may tend to perform more poorly in school. In addition, there may be a detrimental effect on intellectual performance from the father's absence.

Hetherington, Camara, and Featherman (1981) in their comprehensive review find that there are consistent differences favoring children from two-parent families, in achievement and grade point average. However, the differences in achievement are too small to be meaningful. Milne et al. (1986) find that although the total differences are fairly substantial, the negative effects on achievement of living in one-parent families are almost entirely due to intervening variables such as income, mother's employment, parental expectations, and parental help with homework.

Krein and Beller (1988) use matched mother-child data from the NLSY mother-child sample to investigate this hypothesis. They find that the negative effect of living in a single-parent family increases with the number of years spent in this type of family, is greatest during the preschool years, and is larger for boys than girls. Controlling for income does not diminish these effects.

Hanushek (1992) finds somewhat different results—the presence or absence of an adult male in the family appears to have no effect on achievement, once income is held constant. Hill and O'Neill (1993) report that the marital status variables have only weak and statistically insignificant effects on children's test scores, when other factors such as mother's characteristics and family resources are taken into account. Desai, Chase-Lansdale, and Michael (1989) also find that family structure has very little effect on child outcomes, holding other factors constant.

The findings with respect to the effect of family structure on achievement appear to be somewhat mixed but generally do not offer overwhelming support of the common perception that marital disruption or absence of the father has a detrimental effect on achievement.

Family Size

There is a substantial amount of literature on the effects of size of family on achievement. Blake's (1989) main hypothesis is that number of siblings will have a negative effect on child achievement outcomes because of a dilution of familial resources available to children in large families and a concentration of such resources in small ones. The dilution occurs both in divisible resources such as parents' time, emotional and physical energy, attention, and ability to interact with children as individuals, but also in material resources and the environment that these material resources can provide. Being brought up in a large family generally means some dilution in privacy and freedom from impingement by other siblings; it also dilutes children's urgency to associate outside the family group, thus making them more parochial and limited in understanding of a variety of social roles. Additionally, as Zajonc (1976) suggests, the overall intellectual level of the home may become more "childlike" in large families because the presence of young children may inhibit adult conversation, vocabulary, and interests.

Some have argued that family size effects are spurious and are merely measuring additional parental characteristics that have been omitted in the model, such as parental IQ, parental personality characteristics, and parental perceptions of desirable qualities in children (Lindert, 1977). Blake insists that genuine family size effects exist and their magnitude in many cases is substantial. Even after controlling for major parental background characteristics, she finds differences in total educational attainment—approximately two years of schooling—between small and large families. The negative educational effects of large families can be somewhat offset by some forces—such as the Catholic church, kin cohesion among some ethnic groups, high parental socioeconomic status (SES), or a combination of these influences. The analysis also isolated family size effects specifically for verbal ability, which is generally strongly related to parental attention and interaction. The magnitude of the effects of family size on IQ is large, with only children generally doing better than multiple siblings. Children from small families are more likely to engage in intellectual and cultural pursuits, to spend more time playing alone, to be more popular, and to have more confidence in their own ability. She also reexamines Zajonc's explanation of the decline in SAT scores in terms of average birth order and shows that it may have more to do with average family size than birth order.

Hanushek's (1992) underlying conceptual model assumes that parents allocate their time to maximize total or average achievement by their children. Parental time is of two types: "public" time, which all children share and which is in the nature of a public good that can be consumed by all without lowering the amount available to other children; and "private" time, which is child-specific and which, of course, declines as family size becomes larger. Thus, achievement of each child can be expected to fall with the addition of more children. The results confirm the tradeoff between quantity and quality of children. Annual achievement growth of each child in the family falls, but at a declining rate, as family size increases. Within families, birth order appears to have little effect on performance. He also estimates that changes in family size that occurred over the past two decades help explain half or more of the aggregate changes in the sixth-grade Iowa achievement tests over the period 1965 to 1985.

Hill and O'Neill (1993) reinforce these findings: On average, test scores on the Peabody Picture Vocabulary Test (PPVT) fall two points for each additional child and the effect is highly significant.

A more recent study may indicate that a broader perspective is needed than a simple one of children in a family competing for scarce resources. Children may also be considered as resources themselves. For instance, older children may be able to help younger children. The study of the achievement of children of Vietnamese immigrants to the U.S. (Caplan et al., 1991, 1992) shows a positive and significant sign for family size, which is attributed to the fact that in immigrant families especially, older children may be significant resources within the family system.

Educational Attainment of Parents

As we said above, educational attainment of parents may be a proxy for the cognitive abilities of the parents and thus affect the innate endowment of the child. It may also be a proxy for cultural variables such as persistence and emphasis on and taste for learning, all of which should strongly influence the child's achievement. Higher educational attainment has been linked to the provision of a more stimulating home environment and to values that encourage self-direction in a child (Kohn, 1983; Bradley, 1985). Direct tests of the effect of parental educational attainment on children's achievement are few—most studies tend to subsume this variable under the more global variable measuring the family's SES. Hill and O'Neill (1993) explicitly include mother's education and find that an additional year of mother's schooling raises the average PPVT score by about 1.2 percentile points. The importance of this variable diminishes when they control for the number of times the mother reads to the child. However, it is likely that the two are highly correlated and the mother's effectiveness in providing a stimulating, learning environment probably depends partly on level of maternal educational attainment. Menaghan and Parcel (1991) find that mothers with higher levels of schooling provide better home environments, as do mothers with more complex occupations (who tend to have higher schooling as well). An earlier paper (Parcel and Menaghan, 1990) discusses the intergenerational effects of maternal work experiences on children's verbal facility. They argue that mothers who work in occupations with more complex activities tend to provide more enriching home environments than those who work in less complex occupations, and so help develop critical cognitive skills that enhance child achievement.

There is little empirical evidence of the independent effect of paternal educational attainment once family income and mother's education levels are included. We include father's education to better measure the intergenerational transmission of cognitive ability, as well as the cultural environment at home.

Age of Mother at Child's Birth

The age of the mother at a child's birth and test scores are likely to be related, perhaps not directly but because of several intervening factors. The resources parents can devote to their children will vary over time and will influence achievement. However, these effects are likely to depend strongly on family size as well. In addition, young mothers are more likely to be in their teen years, children themselves, with little ability to parent a young child. They are more likely to be unmarried and less educated and, therefore, economically deprived—all of which will affect the educational outcomes of their children. Moore and Snyder (1991) used data from NLSY to examine the effects of early childbearing on the cognitive test scores of three- to seven-year-old firstborn children. The mother's age at the child's birth was less important as a predictor of the child's cognitive score than the mother's score on a test of cognitive achievement. Hill and O'Neill (1993), however, find that the mother's age at the child's birth has a positive and statistically significant effect on children's scores, although Desai et al. (1989) find little effect.

Family Income

The relationship between income or more broadly SES and achievement is fairly well documented. More recently, Hill and O'Neill (1993) find that income has a positive and significant effect on children's test scores: An increase of $10,000 per year would increase scores by 2.4 percentile points, although the effect is nonlinear. Hanushek (1992) finds that permanent income has a systematic effect on achievement, although current income does not, suggesting that a policy of increasing current family income by itself may not translate into higher achievement.

Maternal Employment

The relationship between maternal employment and educational outcomes has been the subject of much heated debate. Some have argued that maternal employment directly decreases the amount of time available for each child and increases the stress on the mother because of the dual role and so has a negative effect on achievement. Others believe that employment can enhance a woman's sense of self-worth and satisfaction with life and will lead to her providing a better home environment.

Leibowitz (1974) finds that the quantity and quality of a mother's time spent in preschool home education have a significant effect on her child's IQ. Milne et al. (1986) find that the significant effects of mother's employment on children's achievement is primarily negative but differs by child's age, race, family structure, and the amount of time the mother works. Gottfried et al. (1988) present research that examines family environmental processes and children's development as related to maternal employment. Their position is that it is the proximal home environment that is important rather than employment status per se. They used a longitudinal dataset that followed children over a seven-year period but did not find any negative effect of maternal employment status on children's development, although the number of hours worked was negatively correlated with achievement measures. However, employed mothers hold higher educational expectations for their children, and higher educational expectations are related to higher cognitive development, academic achievement, and social development.

Hoffman (1989), in a review of the effect of maternal employment in the two-parent family, concludes that maternal employment generally adds to the morale of mothers and that parental attitudes are more important than mother's employment status. Blau and Grossberg (1992) find that although maternal employment has a negative effect on young children's cognitive development during the first year of a child's life, it is potentially offset by a positive effect during the second and subsequent years. Similarly, Desai et al. (1989) find that the overall effect of maternal employment on the intellectual ability of four-year-olds is negligible.

SUMMARY

This chapter briefly illustrates the importance of an integrated framework, drawn from several disciplines, in modeling student achievement. However, it is difficult to find comprehensive data that would allow us to fit such complex models. Given data limitations, we focus in this study on a set of family and demographic variables that are available in several national databases. We review previous studies that show the importance of these variables in explaining differences in student achievement. This set of variables includes family type, family size, age of mother at child's birth, educational attainment of parents, maternal employment status, and race/ethnicity.

Chapter Five

MULTIVARIATE ANALYSIS OF ACHIEVEMENT SCORES

This chapter describes the development of the equations used to predict individual test scores for children ages 14–15 and 15–18.

ANALYSIS VARIABLES

Variable definitions for the analysis variables in the model of student achievement are provided in Table 5.1. The definitions are matched across the two datasets.

The dependent variables in each model are standardized, weighted mathematics and verbal/reading z-scores. These are calculated from the test scores on the mathematics and verbal/reading tests given to the respondents on the two datasets, weighted across all observations. For a sample with mean $\overline{X}$ and standard deviation s, the sample z-score for a particular observation X_i is:

$$z_i = \frac{X_i - \overline{X}}{s}$$

The numerical value of the z-score reflects the relative standing of the observation. The z-score distribution has a mean of 0 and a standard deviation of 1 and thus allows comparisons of performance on different tests. The z-scores can easily be translated into percentile units—a more commonly used measure—using the fact that a standard deviation shift is approximately 34 percentile points, whereas a shift of 0.10 of a standard deviation is a shift of about 3.4 percentile points.

Table 5.1

Variable Definitions

Variable Name	Definition
Dependent variable	
Mathematics score	Weighted, standardized z-score
Verbal score	Weighted, standardized z-score
Independent variables	
Family income	1987 dollars (000s)
Number of siblings	Total number of siblings, aged 18 or younger
Age of mother at	
child's birth	Age of mother at birth of child
Mother's education	
Less than high school	= 1, if education < 12 years
	= 0, otherwise
Some college	= 1, if 13 years ≤education
	≤15 years
	= 0 otherwise
College graduate	= 1, if education ≥16 years
	= 0, otherwise
Father's education	
Less than high school	= 1, if education < 12 years
	= 0, otherwise
Some college	= 1, if 13 years ≤ education
	≤15 years
	= 0, otherwise
College graduate	= 1, if education ≥16 years
	= 0, otherwise
Single mother	= 1, if child lives in a single-parent household, headed by mother
	= 0, otherwise
Mother working	= 1, if mother is in the labor force
	= 0, otherwise
Race/ethnicity	
Black	= 1, if child is black
	= 0, otherwise
Hispanic	= 1, if child is of Hispanic origin
	= 0, otherwise
Female	= 1, if child is female
	= 0 otherwise

Table 5.1 (continued)

Variable Name	Definition
Region dummies	
Northeast	= 1, if child lives in Northeast region
	= 0, otherwise
North Central	= 1, if child lives in North Central region
	= 0, otherwise
West	= 1, if child lives in the West
	= 0, otherwise
Missing value dummies	
Income missing	= 1, if income is missing
	= 0, otherwise
Mother's education missing	= 1, if mother's education is missing
	= 0, otherwise
Father's education missing	= 1, if father's education is missing
	= 0, otherwise
Number of siblings missing	= 1, if number of siblings is missing
	= 0, otherwise
Age of mother missing	= 1, if age of mother is missing
	= 0, otherwise
Type of household missing	= 1, if type of household missing
	= 0, otherwise
Mother's work status missing	= 1, if mother's work status missing
	= 0, otherwise

Most of the independent variables are self-explanatory. Family income is expressed in 1987 constant dollars (000s). Other continuous variables are age of mother at child's birth and number of siblings. The number of siblings used in the analysis includes only siblings who were 18 years old or younger living in the household. Thus, our family size variable will be a better measure for the NELS eighth-grade sample than the NLSY sample of 15–18-year-olds, since the latter sample may have more siblings older than 18.

Because the NELS had only categorical data on parental education, we used dummy variables for characterizing education for both parents. Gender, race/ethnicity, single mother, mother's work status, and region are also all entered as dummy variables. Race/ethnicity is coded as three mutually exclusive groups—black, Hispanic, non-Hispanic white. Mother's working status includes both full- and part-time work and the definitions varied slightly on each survey. On the NLSY survey, the question asked the mother's main activity when the child was age 14, whereas the NELS survey question asked about whether the mother worked full-time during the past week.

Also included is a set of dummies to control for missing data in a number of fields such as income, parental education, age of mother at child's birth, family size, family type, and mother's work status.[1] The set of missing dummy variables is somewhat different for the two datasets because the amount of missing data on given variables was different. This approach increased sample sizes in both surveys.[2] Explicitly controlling for the missing data allows us to see whether these individuals differ from the nonmissing cases in some systematic way.

The weighted and unweighted means and standard deviations for both the NLSY and NELS samples are given in Table 5.2. The large differences in unweighted characteristics and mean test scores reflect two factors. First, the stratification scheme is quite different for the two samples—the NLSY oversampled low-income whites and minorities, both of whom tend to have lower scores on standardized tests; the NELS oversampled private schools, many of which may have higher achieving students. Second, the NLSY was given in 1980 and the NELS in 1988, and shifts in the distribution of particular variables could have occurred over this time period.

---

[1]We included missing value dummies for all cases with missing data but only for those variables for which 3 percent or more of the cases were missing data. In each case, the missing value was replaced with the weighted mean of the variable for all nonmissing cases. In the case of missing parental education, we substituted the education of the other parent, whenever possible, and the weighted mean of the variable itself, whenever spouse education was missing as well. For the NELS, we also substituted student-reported data for missing parent data. This procedure was followed in all cases, regardless of whether the data were missing because the adult respondent in a two-parent household failed to provide information about the other parent or because only one parent was present in the family.

[2]A sensitivity analysis was performed using only the cases with all data present, and results were substantially the same as those obtained by including missing data cases.

Table 5.2

Means and Standard Deviations of the Analysis Variables: Weighted and Unweighted

| | NLSY | | | | NELS | | | |
| | Unweighted | | Weighted | | Unweighted | | Weighted | |
Variable	Mean	S.D.	Mean	S.D.	Mean	S.D.	Mean	S.D.
Income ($1987 000s)	27.91	19.32	33.94	21.04	42.63	41.76	38.78	34.32
Mother's education								
Less than high school	0.48	0.50	0.35	0.48	0.18	0.38	0.18	0.39
Some college	0.08	0.28	0.10	0.31	0.23	0.42	0.24	0.42
College graduate	0.07	0.25	0.10	0.30	0.20	0.40	0.16	0.37
Father's education								
Less than high school	0.49	0.50	0.37	0.48	0.18	0.39	0.19	0.39
Some college	0.08	0.28	0.11	0.31	0.20	0.40	0.21	0.41
College graduate	0.12	0.32	0.17	0.38	0.28	0.45	0.24	0.43
Age of mother at child's birth	26.25	6.48	26.39	6.41	25.88	5.75	25.62	5.75
Number of siblings	3.77	2.58	3.23	2.26	2.25	1.50	2.26	1.50
Single mother	0.21	0.41	0.19	0.35	0.16	0.36	0.17	0.36
Mother working	0.54	0.50	0.56	0.50	0.51	0.48	0.51	0.48
Female	0.49	0.50	0.49	0.50	0.50	0.50	0.50	0.50
Black	0.26	0.44	0.14	0.34	0.12	0.33	0.13	0.34
Hispanic	0.14	0.35	0.05	0.26	0.13	0.34	0.10	0.30
Northeast	0.19	0.39	0.20	0.40	0.20	0.40	0.19	0.39
North Central	0.25	0.43	0.30	0.46	0.26	0.44	0.26	0.44
West	0.18	0.38	0.16	0.37	0.20	0.40	0.19	0.39
Income missing	0.17	0.38	0.19	0.39	0.04	0.20	0.04	0.20
Mother's education missing	0.04	0.19	0.03	0.16	0.02	0.13	0.01	0.12
Father's education missing	0.11	0.32	0.07	0.26	0.07	0.25	0.07	0.25
Age of mother missing	0.05	0.23	0.04	0.20	0.06	0.23	0.06	0.23
Number of siblings missing	—	—	—	—	0.02	0.12	0.01	0.12
Type of household missing	—	—	—	—	0.03	0.18	0.04	0.19
Mother's work status missing	—	—	—	—	0.03	0.17	0.03	0.17
Standardized math score	−0.27	1.02	0.00	1.00	0.06	1.02	0.00	1.00
Standardized verbal score	−0.31	1.07	0.00	1.00	0.05	1.01	0.00	1.00
N	5,343	—	5,343	—	22,915	—	22,915	—

The unweighted average z-score in the NELS sample is 0.06 for mathematics and 0.05 for verbal compared to the mean on the NLSY, which is about a third of a standard deviation below the mean. The average z-score for the weighted samples is, of course, 0 by construction, with a standard deviation of 1. The unweighted income in the NELS sample is 50 percent higher than that of the NLSY respondents, although the weighted means reflect a much smaller difference. Average educational attainment is also considerably higher in the

NELS: Approximately 40 percent of mothers of the NELS eighth-graders have post-high school education compared to 15–20 percent of the mothers in the NLSY sample. The same disparity is evident in the father's schooling level. Family sizes are also significantly smaller in the NELS than NLSY, and there is a somewhat lower proportion of single parents in NELS. The proportion of mothers working does not appear to have changed much. The unweighted NLSY sample, by design, has a much higher proportion of minorities—about 40 percent, compared to the NELS, where only a quarter are black or Hispanic.

Before we present estimation results, we first present differences in simple test score means for different groups. Policy debates and popular commentaries on education and the family often use these simple differences between groups when advocating particular policies. For instance, a great deal of emphasis is given to the lower test scores of children in single-parent families. However, the size and relative magnitude of these effects can be quite misleading if other characteristics are not taken into account. A fairer comparison would be between students in single-parent households and students in two-parent households, who are otherwise similar in other characteristics. This is the advantage of multivariate models. We later compare the univariate relationship with multivariate results to contrast the differences.

SIMPLE DIFFERENCES IN MEAN TEST SCORES FOR SELECTED GROUPS

Figures 5.1 and 5.2 show weighted differences in mean test scores (in standard deviation units) for selected groups of the NELS and NLSY samples. The two samples are very similar with respect to the direction and relative magnitude of the effects of family characteristics on student test scores. The largest differences in both samples occur in children whose parents differ in educational attainment. For example, we find that children of college graduates score about a standard deviation or higher on both verbal/reading and mathematics tests than children whose parents who did not graduate from high school. The next largest differences are between the racial/ethnic groups, with black students scoring 0.75 to 1.25 of a standard deviation lower on mathematics and verbal scores than non-

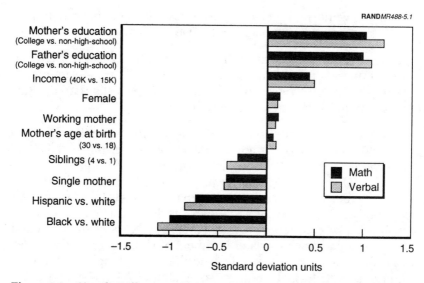

Figure 5.1—Simple Differences in Mean Test Scores for Selected Groups, NLSY

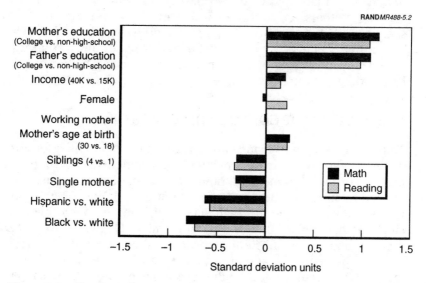

Figure 5.2—Simple Differences in Mean Test Scores for Selected Groups, NELS

Hispanic white students, and Hispanics scoring approximately 0.75 of a standard deviation below non-Hispanic whites.

Income, age of mother at birth of child, family size, and single- versus two-parent family all appear related to student achievement. We find differences of approximately 0.20 to 0.50 of a standard deviation between the different groups in both samples.

Children who come from households with a family income of $40,000 score 0.50 of a standard deviation higher on the NLSY and 0.20 of a standard deviation higher on the NELS compared to children with incomes of $15,000. Children of older mothers (30 years at time of child's birth) score nearly 0.25 of a standard deviation higher on the NELS and 0.10 of a standard deviation higher on the NLSY compared to children of teen mothers (18 years at time of child's birth). Children with greater numbers of siblings do worse on tests by about 0.33 of a standard deviation on both samples. Children in households with single mothers score about 0.40 of a standard deviation lower on the NLSY and about 0.25 of a standard deviation lower on the NELS than children in two-parent households. Children with working mothers versus those with nonworking mothers appear to score no differently on the NELS and slightly higher on the NLSY. The patterns appear very similar for mathematics and verbal tests except for differences by gender, with girls scoring higher on verbal/reading tests on both samples.

THE PROBLEM OF CONFOUNDING FACTORS

To illustrate the point made earlier regarding the potential for erroneous inferences that exists when looking at simple relationships, we use data from the NLSY to examine the characteristics of households headed by single mothers and two-parent households. The proportion of mothers without a high school diploma is much higher in single-parent families than two-parent families (40 percent versus 25 percent) and a much higher porportion of them is black (33 percent versus 8 percent). In addition, their mean income is significantly lower—60 percent lower than the mean in two-parent families. The lower achievement found in children living in single-parent households could be due to these differences rather than to the fact that they are living with a single mother.

Because simple test score differences between groups can be misleading, the next subsection presents the results of the multivariate model that estimates the relative net contribution of each these various factors, controlling for all other family factors.

MULTIVARIATE RESULTS FOR ENTIRE SAMPLE

The models presented here assume a simple linear relationship between test scores and family and demographic characteristics. Subsequent reports will explore the effects of specifying more complex models that specifically test for nonlinearities in the relationships and for interactions between independent variables. We present the unweighted results in the main text.[3]

NLSY Regression Results

Table 5.3 presents the regression estimates for mathematics and verbal scores for all racial/ethnic groups. The regression coefficients are expressed in standard deviation units (or portions of one standard deviation) because the dependent variable in the regression is a z-score. Thus, the coefficient of a given variable represents the effect of a one-unit change in the variable on the standardized test score in standard deviation units. Income, parental education, age of mother at birth of child, number of siblings, working mother, and racial/ethnic variables all are statistically significant with respect to both the mathematics and verbal models.[4]

---

[3]Statisticians appear to be somewhat divided on the appropriateness of conducting weighted versus unweighted regressions. The general consensus is that if the model is correctly specified, then unweighted regressions are efficient (Murnane, 1986; DuMouchel and Duncan, 1983; Lee et al., 1990). For our simple models, we estimated both weighted and unweighted regressions and compared the two, using DuMouchel and Duncan's (1983) procedure. There were no substantive differences between these regressions, except for the effects of race and ethnicity, which were much stronger in the weighted models, as expected, because of stratification of the samples. For predictive purposes, we find that using the weighted coefficients makes little difference to the results reported in Chapter Six.

[4]In testing the null hypothesis that a particular coefficient is not significantly different from 0, one usually uses a critical t-value of 1.96 (p ≤ 0.05). This is based on the conventionally computed standard errors, which assume a simple random sample. Both the NLSY and the NELS are multistage, stratified random samples and respondents tend to be in clusters, which tend to be homogeneous in a variety of

Table 5.3

Regression Results: NLSY

Variable	Mathematics		Verbal	
	Coef.	t-Stat.	Coef.	t-Stat.
Intercept	−0.541	−8.393	−0.533	−8.302
Income	0.0075	10.479	0.0071	9.979
Mother's education				
Less than high school	−0.167	−5.391	−0.255	−8.307
Some college	0.145	3.081	0.143	3.051
College graduate	0.150	2.694	0.177	3.178
Father's education				
Less than high school	−0.190	−6.11	−0.214	−6.916
Some college	0.163	3.451	0.208	4.412
College graduate	0.326	6.961	0.362	7.776
Age of mother	0.011	5.83	0.016	8.55
Number of siblings	−0.043	−8.402	−0.071	−13.701
Single mother	−0.010	−0.297	−0.0043	−0.134
Mother working	0.075	3.085	0.089	3.655
Female	0.165	6.983	0.139	5.917
Black	−0.488	−15.796	−0.546	−17.733
Hispanic	−0.159	−4.116	−0.217	−5.619
Northeast	0.084	2.471	0.134	3.934
North Central	0.191	6.052	0.143	4.563
West	0.025	0.704	0.064	1.774
Income missing	0.0019	0.059	0.016	0.499
Mother's education missing	−0.275	−4.084	−0.272	−4.049
Father's education missing	−0.092	−2.198	−0.124	−2.967
Age of mother missing	0.047	0.881	0.056	1.059
Adjusted R^2	0.2849		0.3595	

Income shows a strong positive relationship to student achievement. This relationship estimates that a $10,000 increase in income would, other things constant, increase test scores by a little less than 0.10 of a standard deviation (0.075) or approximately 2.6 percentile points.

The effect of mother's education is both large and statistically significant. The relationship shows that having a mother who did not

---

ways. This means that the reported standard errors may be too small and the reported t-statistics inflated, leading to incorrect rejection of the null hypothesis. The ratio of the correct standard error to the computed standard error is known as the design effect and one needs to adjust the critical t-value upward by this design effect. Although a single design effect cannot be computed, a rough approximation is 1.5, giving us a critical t-value of approximately 3.00. Although we report the unadjusted t-statistics here, the discussion implicitly uses a critical t-value of 3.00.

complete high school lowers both mathematics and verbal scores by about 0.20 of a standard deviation compared to having a mother who completed high school; having a mother who has some college or is a college graduate increases the score by about 0.15 to 0.18 of a standard deviation.

The effect of father's education is somewhat larger than that of mother's education, even after controlling for mother's education. The relationship shows that having a father who is a college graduate versus one who is a high school graduate increases scores by about 0.40 of a standard deviation for both mathematics and verbal scores—a large change that translates into a difference of about 14 percentile points. Thus, these data indicate that the education level of *both* mothers and fathers is important in accounting for test score differences.

Our family size effects are quite large and statistically significant for mathematics and verbal scores. The results show that each additional sibling lowers a child's achievement by 0.04 to 0.07 of a standard deviation; an easier way to understand this is to note that a child with two siblings will score about 0.10 of a standard deviation lower than a child with no siblings. Family size appears to have stronger effects on verbal scores than on mathematics scores.

We also find a significant positive relationship of age of mother on student achievement—with children of older mothers doing better on standardized tests. A child born to a mother who is 10 years older will score about 0.10 of a standard deviation higher than a child with a younger mother.

The estimated model shows that children with working mothers—other things equal—score slightly higher scores by less than 0.10 of a standard deviation in both mathematics and verbal tests. Being in a single-parent household, holding other things constant, shows essentially no effect on mathematics and verbal scores. This net effect is very different from the gross effect reported earlier.[5] We interpret

---

[5]The underlying assumption here is that we have fully controlled for all characteristics of single-parent families or families with working mothers through our simple specification. If there are interaction terms or clusters of unobservable characteristics, it may well turn out that the effect of being brought up in single-parent households or households with working mothers may well depend on other circumstances not fully

these findings for working mother and single-parent family later in the report.

Other things equal, the model shows that women perform better than men on *both* verbal and mathematics scores and the difference is over 0.10 of a standard deviation. Although women frequently do better than men on verbal/reading tests, the higher mathematics scores are a little surprising and may perhaps be explained by the emphasis on arithmetic computations in the ASVAB as well as the sample stratification, which oversampled minorities. On the whole, minority females tend to perform better than their counterpart males (Bock and Moore, 1984).

The effects of race/ethnicity are significantly reduced in the multivariate model but remain quite large and significant. Other things equal, blacks score about 0.50 of a standard deviation below non-Hispanic whites (about 17 percentile points) and Hispanics score about 0.20 of a standard deviation (or 7 percentile points) lower than non-Hispanic whites. The results are consistent for both mathematics and verbal scores.

Other things equal, children in the Northeast and Midwest tend to perform better than children in the South. This may reflect school effects or cultural effects or some combination of the two.

NELS Regression Results

Table 5.4 presents the estimation results from the NELS. Overall, the pattern of results is similar to that found in the NLSY, in terms of direction and relative magnitude of effects, although some of the coefficients differ in magnitude. Income, education of both parents, age of mother, family size, and racial/ethnic variables all have similar signs and are statistically significant in NELS as well. The mathematics and reading models are quite comparable across the two datasets. For example, we find that family size has a stronger effect on verbal/reading scores than on mathematics scores—a result that holds for

---

captured by the simple linear specification used here. For example, the effect of being in a single-parent family may be different depending on whether the mother is a college graduate or a high school dropout, on whether she values education highly and has high aspirations for her child. We are currently exploring these and related issues.

Table 5.4

Regression Results: NELS

Variable	Mathematics		Reading	
	Coef.	t-Stat.	Coef.	t-Stat.
Intercept	-0.269	-8.418	-0.310	-9.551
Income	0.0024	14.991	0.0015	9.347
Mother's education				
Less than high school	-0.147	-7.8	-0.174	-9.085
Some college	0.136	8.421	0.147	8.973
College graduate	0.394	20.058	0.346	17.329
Father's education				
Less than high school	-0.142	-7.571	-0.143	-7.464
Some college	0.156	9.141	0.157	9.016
College graduate	0.414	22.129	0.348	18.298
Age of mother	0.0069	6.576	0.0079	7.409
Number of siblings	-0.018	-4.505	-0.037	-9.003
Single mother	-0.034	1.883	-0.034	-1.848
Mother working	-0.0034	-0.273	0.0033	0.26
Female	-0.025	-2.188	0.217	18.508
Black	-0.591	-31.522	-0.508	-26.646
Hispanic	-0.338	-18.101	-0.273	-14.432
Northeast	0.083	5.084	0.083	4.979
North Central	0.100	6.544	0.044	2.864
West	0.034	2.059	-0.046	-2.73
Income missing	-0.0026	-0.092	-0.023	-0.773
Mother's education missing	-0.119	-2.483	-0.165	-3.392
Father's education missing	-0.112	-4.336	-0.132	-5.016
Number of siblings missing	-0.127	-2.415	-0.109	-2.041
Age of mother missing	-0.102	-2.782	-0.120	-3.212
Type of household missing	-0.193	-6.008	-0.125	-3.841
Mother's work status missing	-0.060	-1.282	-0.055	-1.148
Adjusted R^2	0.2756		0.2315	

both the NLSY and the NELS samples. Living with a single mother is insignificant in both models and both datasets.

The relative contributions of income and parental education to student achievement are somewhat different in the models estimated from the NLSY and NELS. For example, the income effect in the NELS model is reduced by more than one-half compared to that in the NLSY model. On the other hand, the effect of having a mother with a college degree relative to the omitted category (mothers with high school diplomas) in the NELS is more than double what we had found in the NLSY. The effect of having a father with a college degree is also larger for mathematics.

The negative effect of family size is reduced (by almost half) in the NELS, perhaps because there is not as much variation in family size in the NELS as in the NLSY. The effect of the race/ethnicity variables is also stronger in the NELS compared to the NLSY model, although the difference is not as large for blacks. For Hispanics, this may be because immigration over time has substantially changed the character of the Hispanic population and the more recent immigrants may be more constrained by their environment than were earlier immigrants.

Summarizing these differences, we find that in the NELS models, compared to the NLSY, economic factors and family size are less strongly related to student achievement, whereas the effects of parental educational attainment and race/ethnicity (at least for mathematics) are stronger.[6]

We can suggest several reasons why coefficients are likely to differ across the two datasets. First, it may be that the overall strength of family effects and the relative strength of the individual family variables change with the age of the child. Overall, one would expect the relative effects of family variables to decline as the child gets older and is exposed to more schooling and more influence outside the family (Plomin, 1986).

Second, the differences might be due to the presence of nonlinear or interactive effects for family variables. Because of the very different samples, the estimated coefficients could be biased in different ways. Such biases might arise from the nonlinearities and interactive effects for the two samples because of the extremely different stratification used. For instance, if family size has a nonlinear effect, then the large difference in average family size between the two samples would appear as changes in the linear coefficients.[7]

---

[6]The F-test rejects the hypothesis of equality of the two sets of coefficients. The computed F is 9.6 for the math model and 11.7 for the verbal model. The null hypothesis of equality of coefficients for the NLSY and NELS can, therefore, be rejected at the 0.01 level.

[7]A future report addresses this question of the presence of nonlinear and interactive terms and the sensitivity of our results to them.

Third, the underlying structural relationship may well have changed between 1980 and 1988, the time period spanned by our two datasets. For instance, the weaker role of income in the later study might be explained if quality differences among schools decreased in the later period and the role of income in allowing families to move to better school districts became less important.[8]

Fourth, some effects may be caused by differences in the tests themselves. For example, the stronger effect of race/ethnicity in 1988 in the mathematics model might well be an artifact rather than an underlying structural change in the coefficient, caused by differences between the NELS mathematics test and the mathematics segment of the ASVAB.

Comparing Univariate and Multivariate Results

It might be useful to reexamine the statement we had made earlier that simple group differences can potentially be very misleading. We are now in a position to examine more closely the gross versus net effect of particular family characteristics. We do this by comparing the simple test score differences for selected groups of children with the test score differences that would exist if the children had otherwise similar characteristics but differed in this one variable alone. These latter effects are predicted from the multivariate models discussed above. Figures 5.3–5.6 show the results of such comparisons for the four tests under consideration: NLSY mathematics, NLSY verbal, NELS mathematics, and NELS reading tests.

We find that overall the net effects tend to be much smaller—less than one-half of the gross effect. This is not surprising given that the net effect controls for the effect of other variables and the gross effect takes into account both the characteristic under consideration and all the other characteristics that vary with it. The pattern—the overall importance of effects on test scores—remains much the same, however. Where earlier we had seen differences of over one standard deviation between the test scores of children whose parents

---

[8]We hypothesized that part of the differences between the two models might be due to the oversampling of blacks and Hispanics in the NLSY. However, the weighted regressions show similar differences, so this is not likely the case.

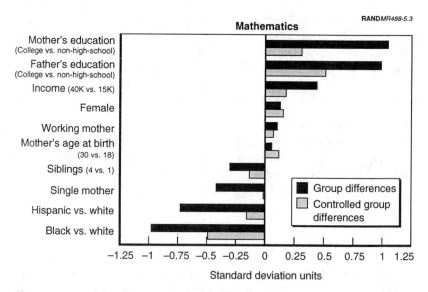

Figure 5.3—Unadjusted Versus Net Differences in Mean Mathematics Test Scores for Selected Groups, NLSY

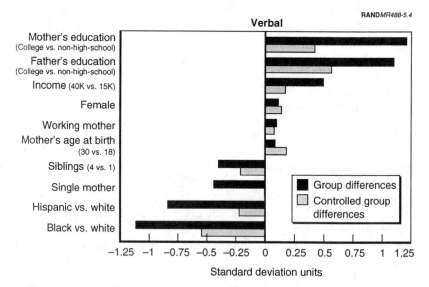

Figure 5.4—Unadjusted Versus Net Differences in Mean Verbal Test Scores for Selected Groups, NLSY

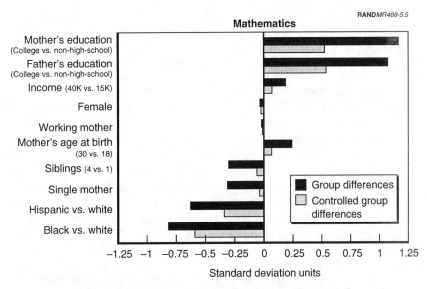

Figure 5.5—Unadjusted Versus Net Differences in Mean Mathematics
Test Scores for Selected Groups, NELS

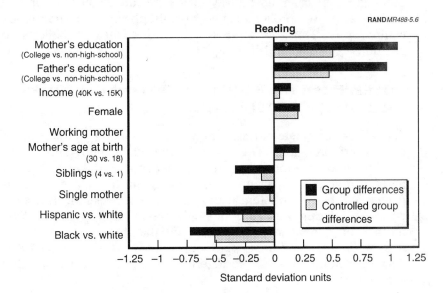

Figure 5.6—Unadjusted Versus Net Differences in Mean Reading
Test Scores for Selected Groups, NELS

did not have a high school diploma and the test scores of those whose parents were college graduates, we now predict differences of between one-quarter and one-half of a standard deviation, which, while large, are not as large as the unadjusted effects.

In particular, notice the effect of being brought up in a female-headed household. The effect is essentially zero, very different from the 0.40 difference seen earlier. Apparently, a lot of the gross difference is indeed due to income, low maternal education levels, and other factors that frequently characterize single-parent families rather than family structure itself. The family effects show that a child with four siblings will score about 0.20 of a standard deviation lower on the verbal/reading test and 0.10 lower on a mathematics test than a child with only one sibling. The differences by race/ethnicity are still quite large but considerably smaller than the gross effect.

Essentially, we see the same patterns for both mathematics and verbal score differences and for the NLSY and NELS samples.

Using gross effects almost always overstates the effect of a variable and in some cases implies an effect that disappears for the controlled comparisons. Thus, use of gross effects for advocating policies on positions can be very misleading.

INTERPRETING THE RESULTS FOR WORKING MOTHERS AND SINGLE-PARENT FAMILIES

The effects of single-parent families and working mothers need careful interpretation. The effects of the other family and demographic variables—income, parental education, family size, age of mother at child's birth, and race/ethnicity—in the analysis are expected and fairly consistent with a long line of research. However, when considering the effects of single-parent families and working mothers on student achievement, we find that the evidence is mixed. It is important, therefore, to place our results in perspective, to highlight their limitations, and to determine the extent of bias in these coefficients.

We find an insignificant effect for single parents in both datasets. For working mothers, we find an insignificant coefficient in one and a small, positive, significant coefficient in the other. These results mirror the mixed findings in the literature cited earlier and are consistent with recent work using different sources of data. For example, Hill and O'Neil (1992) use the child supplement from the NLSY to estimate regressions on test scores for 3–6- and 6–9-year-old children and find similar insignificant effects for single-parent and working-mother variables once other family factors are taken into account. With data from the General Social Surveys from 1974–1990, Alwin (1991) finds insignificant effects of single parents and working mothers on verbal scores when controlling for other family measures.

However, for several reasons one needs to be cautious when interpreting these null or small significant effects. First, when single families are created by divorce, there are usually changes in other family characteristics as well—most notably family income. For instance, average family income significantly declines. So the full effect on test scores of the increase in the number of single-parent families is reflected through a drop in family income as well as a change in the family structure from a single to two parents. The results suggest that after taking account of these changes and other measured differences between single- and two-parent families, we would find no significant added effect on test scores simply from the difference in family structure between single- and two-parent families. However, even this interpretation needs more precision.

A second important consideration is that there might be unmeasured differences in single-parent or working-mother families that may not be reflected in our models. Perhaps the best example is that single-parent families most often result from divorce, and divorce can be preceded by a conflictual family environment, which research shows can be very detrimental to children's development (Demo and Acock, 1988; Demo, 1992). This introduces the possibility that the coefficient reflects the unmeasured characteristics as well as the variable itself. Thus, the absence of an average effect of being in a single-parent family on test scores—other things equal—might reflect the fact that for youth in many of these homes, prior conditions may have been detrimental to achievement. This implies that the result should not be generalized across all families. In simpler terms, some children living with a single parent may be better off than those living with two parents who are in conflict. However, the results do not imply that childen in nonconflictual two-parent families would be equally well off in a single-parent family.

Third, perhaps the most important consideration is that the effects of working mothers and being in a single-parent family may vary considerably depending on the family context. These effects are likely to differ by family size, by educational level of parents, or by income level. Thus, an insignificant coefficient for working mothers or single parents may well hide offsetting strong positive and negative effects in different types of families.[9] However, our results provide some evidence that, when looking at average effects across all families, neither the potential positive nor negative effects of working-mother or single-parent families dominate. This again means that the results cannot be generalized to all types of families.

An important limitation of our analysis is that we measured maternal labor-force participation and family type when the child was approximately 14 years old. This does not account for whether the mother was working at younger ages or how long the single-parent status existed. It may be important to distinguish between children who have been in single-parent families from birth and those who have lived a significant part of their life in a two-parent household. In the latter case, the level of family income may have been much higher during a portion of the child's life, and the current family income may be a poor proxy for the family resources available earlier.

REGRESSION RESULTS BY RACIAL/ETHNIC GROUP

We had seen earlier that the race/ethnicity dummy variables were large and statistically significant in our total regressions. Introducing race/ethnicity by means of dummy variables presupposes that the achievement process for blacks and Hispanics does not differ from that for non-Hispanic whites other than in the constant term. However, to test more precisely this assumption of equality across the three groups (blacks, Hispanics, and non-Hispanic whites), we esti-

---

[9]We have run models that fully interact all variables and we do find that single parents and working mothers can have strong interaction terms in the positive or negative direction.

mated separate regressions for each and then used an F-test to test for stability of the coefficients across the groups.

Table 5.5 provides the unweighted means of the analysis variables for the three groups for both the NLSY and the NELS datasets.[10] As

Table 5.5

Means of the Analysis Variables for Race/Ethnicity Models

Variable	NLSY Non-Hispanic Whites	NLSY Blacks	NLSY His-panics	NELS Non-Hispanic Whites	NELS Blacks	NELS His-panics
Income ($1987 000s)	33.40	19.64	21.77	48.06	23.43	26.93
Mother's education						
Less than high school	0.35	0.56	0.79	0.12	0.21	0.45
Some college	0.10	0.07	0.04	0.24	0.26	0.17
College graduate	0.09	0.04	0.02	0.22	0.12	0.08
Father's education						
Less than high school	0.39	0.58	0.74	0.14	0.22	0.45
Some college	0.10	0.06	0.04	0.21	0.19	0.17
College graduate	0.16	0.05	0.04	0.32	0.15	0.12
Age of mother at child's birth	26.41	25.96	26.24	25.95	24.77	25.63
Number of siblings	3.21	4.60	4.55	2.10	2.65	2.76
Single mother	0.14	0.38	0.21	0.13	0.39	0.18
Mother working	0.53	0.59	0.47	0.49	0.57	0.47
Female	0.49	0.49	0.52	0.50	0.51	0.52
Northeast	0.20	0.15	0.19	0.21	0.19	0.14
North Central	0.32	0.19	0.07	0.30	0.19	0.12
West	0.16	0.06	0.48	0.15	0.07	0.41
Income missing	0.19	0.16	0.14	0.04	0.05	0.05
Mother's education missing	0.03	0.06	0.04	0.01	0.02	0.03
Father's education missing	0.06	0.21	0.14	0.04	0.18	0.10
Age of mother missing	0.04	0.08	0.04	0.05	0.07	0.08
Number of siblings missing	NA	NA	NA	0.01	0.02	0.04
Type of household missing	NA	NA	NA	0.02	0.08	0.04
Mother's work status missing	NA	NA	NA	0.03	0.04	0.04
Standardized math score	0.02	−0.80	−0.54	0.23	−0.61	−0.43
Standardized verbal score	0.04	−0.92	−0.65	0.22	−0.52	−0.39
N	3,080	1,400	748	15,733	2,860	2,988

---

[10]Because race/ethnicity was one of the primary stratification variables and we are examining each group separately, we report only the unweighted means here.

is clear from the table, family characteristics differ markedly across the three groups. Hispanics and blacks tend to have much lower incomes (about a third lower in the NLSY sample, and about 45 percent lower in the NELS sample) than non-Hispanic whites. Hispanics and blacks also trail non-Hispanic whites in terms of parental educational attainment. Over three-quarters of Hispanic mothers in the NLSY sample and 45 percent in the NELS sample did not have a high school diploma. The same trends are evident with respect to father's educational attainment. Family size also differs across the groups, with non-Hispanic whites having the smallest family size, although the differences have narrowed considerably by 1988, the time when the NELS data were collected. The proportion of single mothers is higher among the minority groups in both samples. The regional pattern reveals that the largest proportion of blacks live in the South, whereas Hispanics are concentrated in the West.

In general, the model results for the three groups show similar patterns as the total sample regression in terms of signs, but somewhat lower significance for the smaller minority samples. However, the sizes of the coefficients of some variables differ across the three groups, and in general, these differences hold across both the mathematics and verbal/reading equations.[11]

Regression Results by Racial/Ethnic Group: NELS

We discuss the NELS results first because the sample sizes for the minority groups are significantly larger for the NELS than for the NLSY and the pattern of differences is clearer. Tables 5.6 and 5.7 present the results of estimating separate race/ethnicity regressions for the mathematics and reading models for the NELS sample.

Mathematics Model. The magnitude of the income coefficient tends to be much greater and that of the parental education coefficients much smaller for the minority groups compared with the non-Hispanic white group.   The effects of age of mother are fairly similar across all three groups, but family size becomes small and

---

[11]The F-test test for homogeneity of coefficients across the three groups was rejected at the 0.01 level. The computed F-statistics were very large: 78.76 for the math model and 61.05 for the verbal model.

Table 5.6

Regression Results by Race/Ethnicity, Mathematics Model: NELS

Variable	Non-Hispanic Whites Coef.	t-Stat.	Blacks Coef.	t-Stat.	Hispanics Coef.	t-Stat.
Intercept	−0.251	−6.32	−0.908	−12.07	−0.496	−5.83
Income	0.00204	11.33	0.0066	8.64	0.0051	7.26
Mother's education						
Less than high school	−0.241	−9.71	−0.118	−2.63	−0.017	−0.40
Some college	0.152	7.95	0.092	2.22	0.106	2.14
College graduate	0.426	18.67	0.284	4.83	0.223	3.23
Father's education						
Less than high school	−0.182	−7.49	−0.047	−1.08	−0.156	−3.65
Some college	0.179	8.78	0.022	0.49	0.106	2.08
College graduage	0.429	19.57	0.283	5.33	0.266	4.32
Age of mother at child's birth	0.0055	4.13	0.0039	1.65	0.0045	1.68
Number of siblings	−0.017	−3.26	−0.0038	−0.42	−0.025	−2.40
Single mother	0.0020	0.08	−0.0095	−0.26	0.0046	0.10
Mother working	−0.023	−1.53	0.026	0.76	0.0039	0.11
Female	−0.017	−1.23	0.0087	0.29	−0.079	−2.54
Northeast	0.115	5.87	0.0056	0.14	−0.069	−1.40
North Central	0.137	7.75	0.0076	0.19	−0.036	−0.68
West	0.027	1.23	−0.021	−0.35	−0.069	−1.91
Income missing	0.017	0.48	0.013	0.18	−0.112	−1.52
Mother's education missing	−0.105	−1.57	−0.138	−1.30	−0.046	−0.48
Father's education missing	−0.134	−3.55	−0.033	−0.77	−0.174	−2.92
Number of siblings missing	−0.333	−4.20	0.213	2.03	0.039	0.37
Age of mother missing	−0.083	−1.62	−0.208	−2.82	−0.102	−1.15
Type of household missing	−0.249	−5.41	−0.056	−1.00	−0.206	−2.56
Mother's work status missing	−0.079	−1.22	0.034	0.34	−0.043	−0.41
Adjusted R^2	0.217		0.122		0.114	

insignificant for the black sample. The effects of single mother and mother working tend to be small and insignificant for all groups. The regional variables tend to show different effects for the three groups. The Northeast and Midwest variables tend to be large and positive for non-Hispanic whites, with the South being lowest. The black sample shows no significant regional effects, whereas the Hispanic sample shows negative but insignificant effects for all regions but the South.

Table 5.7

Regression Results by Race/Ethnicity, Reading Model: NELS

Variable	Non-Hispanic Whites		Blacks		Hispanics	
	Coef.	t-Stat.	Coef.	t-Stat.	Coef.	t-Stat.
Intercept	−0.270	−6.71	−1.103	−13.52	−0.477	−5.37
Income	0.0010	5.56	0.0056	6.90	0.0039	5.31
Mother's education						
Less than high school	−0.226	−9.01	−0.158	−3.24	−0.073	−1.68
Some college	0.147	7.62	0.156	3.47	0.168	3.25
College graduate	0.369	15.92	0.296	4.64	0.223	3.08
Father's education						
Less than high school	−0.182	−7.40	−0.029	−0.63	−0.157	−3.53
Some college	0.181	8.78	0.057	1.17	0.121	2.27
College graduage	0.367	16.52	0.269	4.66	0.209	3.25
Age of mother at child's birth	0.007	5.36	0.0095	3.73	0.0056	1.98
Number of siblings	−0.040	−7.81	0.0042	0.42	−0.046	−4.18
Single mother	−0.012	−0.52	−0.010	−0.25	−0.036	−0.76
Mother working	−0.019	−1.25	0.044	1.19	−0.0081	−0.22
Female	0.233	16.50	0.234	7.17	0.138	4.27
Northeast	0.088	4.43	0.086	1.97	−0.0071	−0.14
North Central	0.048	2.66	0.061	1.41	−0.047	−0.85
West	−0.015	−0.67	−0.109	−1.70	−0.099	−2.63
Income missing	0.0015	0.04	−0.077	−0.98	−0.136	−1.78
Mother's education missing	−0.125	−1.87	−0.131	−1.13	−0.143	−1.43
Father's education missing	−0.135	−3.52	−0.067	−1.44	−0.148	−2.37
Number of siblings missing	−0.211	−2.66	0.142	1.26	−0.074	−0.69
Age of mother missing	−0.126	−2.42	−0.191	−2.39	−0.011	−0.12
Type of household missing	−0.076	−1.63	−0.121	−2.00	−0.107	−1.29
Mother's work status missing	−0.094	−1.44	0.026	0.24	0.0014	0.01
Adjusted R^2	0.177		0.124		0.112	

Reading Model. The reading model results, with some specific exceptions, are quite similar to the mathematics model results.[12] The patterns for income, education, age of mother at child's birth, and family size are all similar to those noted in the mathematics model. The effects of single parent and working mother are small and insignificant, as in the mathematics model. The regional patterns are similar but less pronounced for the non-Hispanic whites. Unlike in

---

[12]The F-test for homogeneity of coefficients across the three groups for the separate math and verbal models rejected the null hypothesis of equality across the groups at the 0.01 level.

the mathematics model, blacks display a regional pattern similar to that of non-Hispanic whites.

The Hispanic regional coefficients show a similar pattern to those of the mathematics models, with negative coefficients for all regions except the South. However, the verbal equation has a somewhat larger negative effect for the West and a smaller negative effect for the Northeast.

Regression Results by Racial/Ethnic Group: NLSY

Mathematics Model. Tables 5.8 and 5.9 show the regression results by race/ethnicity for mathematics and verbal test scores for the NLSY sample. The distinct patterns on education and income noted for the NELS do not show up in the NLSY sample. In general, the size of the income coefficients show much more similarity in the NLSY than in the NELS sample. However, the parental education coefficients show a more pronounced effect for the non-Hispanic whites than for minorities—similar to the NELS. The age of mother at child's birth and family size variables show somewhat stronger effects for non-Hispanic whites than for either minority group. Mother working also shows a statistically significant positive effect for non-Hispanics but insignificant effects for minority groups. Single mother is insignificant for all groups. The regional patterns of the NLSY for the Hispanic and non-Hispanic groups are similar but more pronounced than those of the NELS.

Verbal Model. The effects of all four main family variables—education, parental education, age of mother at child's birth, and family size—are similar across groups in the verbal NLSY model. The coefficients of single mother are small and insignificant across all groups, whereas the effect of mother working is again positive and significant for non-Hispanics. Regional patterns are also similar to the mathematics model, with minor exceptions.

Table 5.8

Regression Results by Race/Ethnicity, Mathematics Model: NLSY

Variable	Non-Hispanic Whites		Blacks		Hispanics	
	Coef.	t-Stat.	Coef.	t-Stat.	Coef.	t-Stat.
Intercept	−0.535	−6.26	−1.109	−9.67	−0.279	−1.50
Income	0.0071	8.21	0.0067	3.87	0.0070	3.00
Mother's education						
Less than high school	−0.242	−6.14	−0.036	−0.63	−0.085	−0.88
Some college	0.129	2.28	0.145	1.50	0.290	1.57
College graduate	0.144	2.22	0.216	1.73	−0.182	−0.72
Father's education						
Less than high school	−0.228	−5.65	−0.087	−1.51	−0.252	−2.77
Some college	0.129	2.28	0.229	2.24	0.189	1.12
College graduage	0.290	5.36	0.330	2.73	0.014	0.08
Age of mother at child's birth	0.014	5.61	0.0067	1.94	−0.000017	−0.0030
Number of siblings	−0.067	−8.58	−0.023	−2.76	−0.036	−2.84
Single mother	−0.065	−1.37	0.080	1.58	−0.000036	0.00
Mother working	0.121	3.81	0.033	0.70	0.034	0.51
Female	0.161	5.15	0.163	3.64	0.143	2.26
Northeast	0.168	3.72	−0.043	−0.67	−0.193	−2.01
North Central	0.227	5.67	0.172	2.89	−0.110	−0.79
West	0.0083	0.17	0.095	0.95	−0.014	−0.18
Income missing	0.042	1.05	0.012	0.19	−0.220	−2.41
Mother's education missing	−0.500	−4.75	−0.117	−1.13	−0.227	−1.36
Father's education missing	−0.100	−1.39	−0.171	−2.79	−0.068	−0.69
Age of mother missing	0.029	0.37	0.099	1.19	−0.0071	−0.04
Adjusted R^2	0.242		0.100		0.102	

SUMMARY

The results from the NLSY and NELS models are substantively similar in the direction and relative significance of family and demographic characteristics for both mathematics and verbal/reading abilities. We find that family income, parental education, age of mother at child's birth, and number of siblings all have statistically significant effects on student achievement and are in the expected direction. The effect of working mother is positive but small. Family structure (single-parent versus two-parent families) is insignificant in both the NLSY and NELS models, after controlling for other variables.

Table 5.9

Regression Results by Race/Ethnicity, Verbal Model: NLSY

Variable	Non-Hispanic Whites		Blacks		Hispanics	
	Coef.	t-Stat.	Coef.	t-Stat.	Coef.	t-Stat.
Intercept	–0.443	–5.43	–1.276	–10.49	–0.332	–1.67
Income	0.0062	7.46	0.0069	3.75	0.0085	3.39
Mother's education						
Less than high school	–0.303	–8.05	–0.147	–2.41	–0.271	–2.62
Some college	0.079	1.46	0.230	2.24	0.339	1.72
College graduate	0.176	2.83	0.314	2.36	–0.218	–0.81
Father's education						
Less than high school	–0.240	–6.22	–0.107	–1.74	–0.332	–3.42
Some college	0.198	3.65	0.241	2.23	0.173	0.96
College graduage	0.372	7.21	0.410	3.20	0.028	0.15
Age of mother at child's birth	0.016	6.64	0.014	3.92	0.014	2.71
Number of siblings	–0.080	–10.72	–0.053	–5.92	–0.084	–6.22
Single mother	–0.041	–0.89	0.053	0.99	–0.032	–0.35
Mother working	0.114	3.75	0.071	1.41	0.058	0.82
Female	0.149	4.97	0.149	3.14	0.044	0.65
Northeast	0.127	2.95	0.187	2.72	–0.152	–1.48
North Central	0.142	3.72	0.213	3.38	–0.228	–1.54
West	0.073	1.58	0.059	0.55	–0.095	–1.15
Income missing	0.021	0.53	0.046	0.70	–0.061	–0.62
Mother's education missing	–0.490	–4.88	–0.161	–1.46	–0.243	–1.36
Father's education missing	–0.127	–1.86	–0.219	–3.37	0.053	0.50
Age of mother missing	–0.0080	–0.11	0.176	2.01	–0.094	–0.54
Adjusted R^2	0.289		0.180		0.182	

There are some differences between the NLSY and NELS results. We find that in the NELS models, compared to those of the NLSY, family income and size are less strongly related to student achievement, but the effect of parental educational attainment and race/ethnicity (at least for mathematics) is stronger. These differences may be partially explained by the differences in the tests given to the two samples, the sampling design, the age spans of the sampled children, and the time period.

In addition to regressions for the total or pooled sample, we fit separate models by race/ethnicity—blacks, Hispanics, non-Hispanic whites. In both the NLSY and NELS, the effects of family characteristics on student achievement do not differ substantially across the three groups from what we found in the model fit to the pooled sample, although, in general, income appeared to be more important for minorities than for non-Hispanic whites, and parental education somewhat less so. The effects of single mother and working mother are generally small and insignificant across all models, although we remain cautious about interpreting these effects too literally without further exploration of interaction terms and nonlinearities in the model specification. We mentioned above that the effects of family structure and maternal labor-force participation may well differ, depending on other family circumstances and environment.

Chapter Six

ESTIMATING THE EFFECTS OF CHANGING FAMILY AND DEMOGRAPHIC CHARACTERISTICS ON TEST SCORES

In this chapter, we first review the methodology used in predicting test scores for samples of young people selected from the CPS files and the assumptions underlying that methodology. We then present differences in estimated mean test scores based on the distributions of predicted test scores for 1970–1990 and for 1975–1990; these differences represent our estimates of the effects of changing family and demographic characteristics on student achievement. We calculate test scores for verbal/reading and mathematics using the NELS equations for 13–14-year-olds and the NLSY equations for 15–18-year-olds. We use two different equations to calculate test scores for the three racial/ethnic groups, based on what we referred to earlier as the "pooled" and "nonpooled" estimates. The former controls for race/ethnicity by dummy variables and was fit to the full sample from the NLSY and the NELS; the "nonpooled" estimates are derived by fitting separate regressions to the samples of blacks, Hispanics, and non-Hispanic whites.

ESTIMATING EFFECTS USING THE CPS SAMPLE

Three important assumptions underlie our methodology:

- structural changes in model coefficients over time are small;

- the estimated coefficients for the family variables would not change appreciably if nonfamily variables were included in the models; and

- cross-sectional estimates of coefficients can accurately estimate the effects of time series changes in the independent variables.

The first assumption implies that models fit to data collected from representative samples of similarly aged students in 1970 and 1990 would produce fairly similar coefficients (see Appendix A for a discussion of this assumption). This assumption could be tested if we had data on family characteristics and test scores of representative samples of similarly aged youth at two points in time. Then the shift in structural coefficients could be estimated, as discussed in Appendix A, and precise estimates of the effect of family and demographic characteristics on test scores could be made.[1]

The NELS and NLSY samples represent data that are eight years apart but cannot be used to estimate shifts in coefficients because of the different age groups, stratification, and tests given to the samples. Earlier, we showed that there are differences in the models fit to the two datasets, and to some extent these differences may reflect structural changes in the coefficients over time. However, despite the differences in the models, we find the overall predictions to be remarkably similar, suggesting that, at least for purposes of estimating family effects, the differences may not be that important.

The second assumption is that the family coefficients that would be estimated from a fully specified and estimated model would be similar to those that include family effects alone. Preliminary evidence with estimating models including school and community factors shows little change in family coefficients.

The third assumption, common to most models based on cross-sectional data, implies that cross-sectional coefficients are similar to coefficients estimated from pooled time-series/cross-sectional data (if such data were available). Cross-sectional coefficients can differ because they measure long-term effects, whereas coefficients emerging from time-series analysis include both short- and long-term effects. In general, it is difficult to make predictions regarding the direction and magnitude of such bias (Kuh, 1959).

---

[1]A test of this hypothesis will be possible when the 1992 Senior NELS sample becomes available. It can be compared to the 1972 Senior sample of the High School and Beyond Survey. However, even preliminary evidence from a comparison of the 1980 and 1990 High School and Beyond Survey and NELS Sophomore sample shows no statistically significant change in SES variables between these samples (Rasinski et al., 1993).

These assumptions enable us to use our estimated equations to predict test scores for samples of children, based on their family and demographic characteristics. We used the March Current Population Surveys to select 14–18-year-olds in a given year: 1970, 1975,[2] and 1990. Second, for each child in the sample, we linked their record to family records that captured family characteristics for the selected sample. These characteristics included race/ethnicity, gender, age of mother at child's birth, parental educational attainment, total family income, type of family (single versus two parent), mother's employment status, family size, and regional variables. Third, we used the equations from the overall NLSY and the NELS models to predict a test score for each child on the CPS files, based on that individual's own family characteristics. We use the NLSY model to predict scores for 15–18-year-olds and the NELS to predict scores for the 14–15-year-olds.[3]

For the longer time period (1970 to 1990), we were able to identify only two racial groups: black and nonblack. Therefore, for these predictions, the full model was estimated on the pooled sample, omitting the Hispanic variable and grouping the Hispanics with the non-Hispanic whites. This provided the pooled estimates. Separate regressions were fit for blacks and nonblacks—these are the non-pooled estimates.

Next, we predicted test scores for 1975 and 1990 for the three racial/ethnic groups, using both the pooled (with the Hispanic variable) and nonpooled estimates (fit to the three groups separately).

This allows us (a) to examine the results separately for the three groups and (b) to compute a weighted overall predicted test score using these separate regression coefficients to see whether this differs from the one predicted by the total pooled prediction equation.

---

[2]We chose 1975 because the identification of Hispanics as a separate group did not begin until after 1970. Thus, all predictions by race/ethnicity are for the years 1975 and 1990, although the predictions for the total sample and for blacks and nonblacks are for the years 1970 and 1990.

[3]The weighted age distribution of the eighth graders on NELS showed that approximately 95 percent of them were 14–15 years old in the spring of 1988. We, therefore, restricted our prediction sample from the CPS to 14–15-year-olds to more closely match the NELS sample.

ESTIMATES OF FAMILY AND DEMOGRAPHIC EFFECTS

Using the Pooled Sample Model: 1970–1990

Figure 6.1 shows the estimated difference in the weighted mean verbal/reading and mathematics test scores (in standard deviation units) for 15–18-year-olds (based on the NLSY model) and 14–15-year-olds (based on the NELS models) from 1970 to 1990 as a result of changing family and demographic factors. We estimate a gain in mathematics test scores of 0.20 of a standard deviation or an increase of about 7–8 percentile points for both age groups. The estimated verbal gains are slightly higher than the mathematics gains (0.25 of a standard deviation) for the 15–18-year-olds, although we predict the same gain in reading for the 14–15-year-olds as in mathematics.

The estimated gains in test scores are somewhat surprising, given the conventional wisdom that the family environment has become steadily worse for children. However, the results are explained when we examine the changes in family and demographic characteristics that occurred between 1970 and 1990 for young people aged 15–18

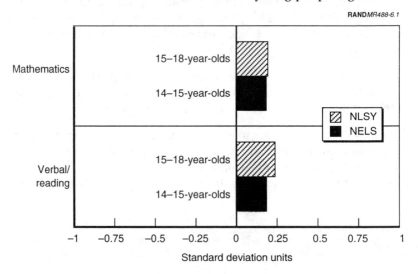

Figure 6.1—Change in Mean Predicted Test Scores Using Estimated Overall Family and Demographic Effects and Pooled Regressions, 1970–1990

(derived from the CPS data) and the strength and significance of the variables in the achievement equations.[4]

Table 6.1 illustrates graphically how we compute the total net effect of changes in selected family characteristics on predicted test scores from 1970 to 1990. The net effect of all these changes in family and demographic characteristics is an estimated *gain* in test scores over this time period primarily as a result of better educated parents and smaller family size.

Table 6.2 presents selected family characteristics for children aged 15–18 in 1970 and 1990. As can be seen from the table, two important trends favor higher achievement—the substantial changes in the educational attainment of both fathers and mothers of adolescents between 1970 and 1990, and the decline in family size. For example, approximately 40 percent of parents had less than a high school education in 1970; this was true of fewer than one-fifth of the parents in 1990. Conversely, the proportion of mothers with some college or a college degree more than doubled over this time period, increasing from 17 percent to 36 percent; for fathers, the

Table 6.1

Estimating the Net Effect of Changing Family Factors

Family Factor	Change (1975–1990)	Net Influence on Test Scores	Combined Effect on Test Scores[a]
Parental education	Large	Large	Large ↑
Family size	Large	Medium	Medium ↑
Family income	None	Medium	None
Mother's age at child's birth	Small	Medium	Small ↓
Working mother	Large	Small	Small ↑
Single parent	Large	None	None

[a]Up arrow indicates net positive effect on scores and down arrow indicates net negative effect on scores.

---

[4]Because the trends are very similar, we do not show the changes in family characteristics of 14–15-year-olds separately in the main body of the report. These are given in Table B.1.

Table 6.2

Selected Family and Demographic Characteristics of 15–18-Year-Olds, 1970–1990

Variable	1970	1980	1990	% Change (1970–1990)
Income ($1987)	38,716	40,531	39,966	+3
Mother's education				
Less than high school	38.2	27.4	17.1	–55
High school	44.7	46.8	47.1	+5
Some college	10.4	15.1	20.0	+92
College graduate	6.7	10.7	15.8	+136
Father's education				
Less than high school	42.8	30.4	19.1	–55
High school	32.7	35.3	37.8	+16
Some college	11.3	15.7	20.3	+80
College graduate	13.2	18.5	22.8	+73
Number of siblings				
0–1	48.2	58.7	72.5	+50
2–3	33.7	32.7	23.5	–30
4 or more	18.0	8.6	4.0	–78
Age of mother at child's birth				
≤19 years	9.3	10.0	13.1	+41
20–24 years	28.2	32.3	31.9	+13
25–29 years	30.9	29.2	33.9	+10
≥30 years	31.6	28.5	21.2	–33
Single mother	13.6	20.0	22.8	+68
Mother working	49.3	59.3	68.6	+39
Race				
Black	11.9	13.7	14.0	+18
Nonblack	88.1	86.3	86.0	–2

increase was from 25 percent in 1970 to 43 percent in 1990. Similarly, there were marked changes in family size over this time period, with smaller families having one to two children becoming more the norm than was previously the case. For example, the number of children with one or no siblings increased from 48 percent in 1970 to 73 percent in 1990; the proportion of children with four or more siblings declined by over 75 percent.

These factors are primarily responsible for the estimated gains, but other factors had small effects. The proportion of children with working mothers increased by about 40 percent and income increased very slightly from 1970 to 1990 by about 3 percent; each makes small positive contributions. However, the small gain in family income reflects several influences.   Income for men—especially younger men—has generally declined in real terms during this period. Family income has been maintained by more mothers working. Another influence on the average family income is the formation of more single-parent families, which often experience income declines in a transition from a two- to a single-parent household.

However, other trends have less favorable effects on achievement. For example, there is an increase in the number of young mothers, from 9 percent in 1970 to 13 percent in 1990; this had a small negative effect on test scores. The proportion of children living with single mothers increased by almost 65 percent over this time period, although the net estimated effect of this variable was seen to be rather small in the models presented earlier. In our methodology, we take account of the increase in single-parent families partially through the family income variable. Presumably, if the number of single-parent families had not increased, family income would have shown stronger gains.

In addition, the racial composition of children changed as the proportion of blacks increased by about 18 percent. This demographic shift—other things equal—would tend to lower scores.

Predicted Changes in Test Scores by Race, 1970–1990

There is considerable interest in how black children have performed over time and whether the gap between blacks and nonblacks has widened or become smaller. Figure 6.2 shows estimates of separate family effects for blacks and nonblacks using the pooled equations.

The black estimates show *greater* gains as a result of changing family factors in *both* mathematics and verbal scores over this time period for both age groups compared to those for whites. Using the NLSY model, we estimate a gain of over 0.30 of a standard deviation in mathematics and 0.40 of a standard deviation in verbal scores for blacks, compared to 0.20 of a standard deviation in mathematics and about 0.25 of a standard deviation in verbal scores for nonblacks. The NELS estimated differences are somewhat smaller than those of the NLSY by about 0.06–0.09 standard deviation units.

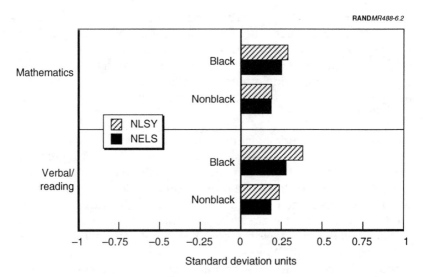

Figure 6.2—Differences in Mean Predicted Test Scores by Race, 1970–1990

One reason for this differential gain between blacks and nonblacks is shown in Table 6.3, which compares changes in black and nonblack families of 15–18-year-olds between 1970 and 1990. Black family characteristics show even more favorable changes than those in nonblack families in the two key areas of parental education and family size.

For example, although the proportion of black mothers with some college increased threefold from 7 percent in 1970 to 25 percent in 1990, the increase among nonblack mothers, although still substantial, was smaller. The same trend is evident among fathers as well. The proportion of black fathers with some college or a college degree increased by almost 300 percent, from 6.5 percent in 1970 to almost 25 percent in 1990, whereas the proportionate increase among nonblack fathers was about 70 percent. The other large contributing factor is the marked decline in family size among blacks. The number of children in small black families increased over 100 percent in this time period compared to a 45 percent increase among nonblack children.

Table 6.3

Profile of Black and Nonblack 15–18-Year-Olds, 1970–1990

Variable	Black				Nonblack			
	1970	1980	1990	% Change (1970– 1990)	1970	1980	1990	% Change (1970– 1990)
Income ($1987)	23,287	23,121	24,068	+3	40,805	43,290	42,545	+4
Mother's education								
Less than high school	63.6	45.8	23.8	–63	34.7	24.5	16.0	–54
High school	29.4	39.1	51.4	+75	46.7	48.0	46.4	–1
Some college	3.9	10.9	17.0	+336	11.3	15.8	20.5	+81
College graduate	3.1	4.2	7.8	+52	7.2	11.8	17.1	+38
Father's education								
Less than high school	72.1	52.2	27.4	–62	38.8	26.9	17.8	–54
High school	21.4	33.8	48.1	+125	34.2	35.6	36.1	+6
Some college	4.0	10.5	15.3	+283	12.3	16.6	21.1	+72
College graduate	2.5	3.5	9.2	+268	14.6	20.9	25.0	+71
Number of siblings								
0–1	30.8	47.1	66.2	+115	50.6	60.6	73.5	+45
2–3	33.2	34.1	26.9	–19	33.8	32.4	23.0	–32
4 or more	36.0	18.8	7.0	–81	15.6	7.0	3.5	–78
Age of mother at child's birth								
≤19 years	15.1	16.6	25.3	+68	8.5	8.9	11.1	+31
20–24 years	26.7	33.1	29.6	+11	28.4	32.2	32.2	+13
25–29 years	28.0	23.6	24.2	–14	31.3	30.0	35.5	+13
≥30 years	30.3	26.6	20.9	–31	31.8	28.8	21.2	–33
Single mother	36.1	52.1	53.3	+48	10.6	14.9	17.9	+69
Mother working	54.0	56.5	67.5	+25	48.7	59.8	68.7	+41

However, two other possible reasons for the black/nonblack differences are use of pooled equations, which assume that black and nonblack coefficients are the same (with the exception of a shift in the constant term), and the inclusion of Hispanics with the nonblack sample.[5] The continuing immigration of Hispanic families could be a factor in lowering the gains of nonblacks. To test these hypotheses, we calculated test scores using race-specific equations for black, Hispanic, and non-Hispanic whites for the period 1975–1990.

---

[5]A third possible reason for the black/nonblack difference is the use of unweighted regression models. We tested this by examining the predictions from our weighted regressions against those from the unweighted models. There was little or no difference in the change in the mean predicted test score between 1970 and 1990.

Estimates for Black, Hispanic, and Non-Hispanic Whites, 1975–1990

Figure 6.3 shows the nonpooled estimates for family effects for blacks, Hispanics, and non-Hispanic whites between 1975 and 1990. For 15–18-year-olds, we predict a gain of about one-quarter of a standard deviation in mathematics and verbal scores for non-Hispanic whites; a gain of 0.15 in mathematics and 0.25 in verbal for blacks. Hispanics show the smallest predicted gain, only 1/20th of a standard deviation in both mathematics and verbal scores. The gains predicted for the 14–15-year-olds have similar patterns across groups but are somewhat smaller for all three groups compared to the NLSY predictions.

The results indicate that some of the black/nonblack results were due to the influence of the expanding Hispanic population as well as the use of pooled models. When we separate Hispanics from the nonblack population, the largest family effects are for the non-Hispanic white group except for the NLSY verbal results, where blacks and non-Hispanic whites show identical gains.

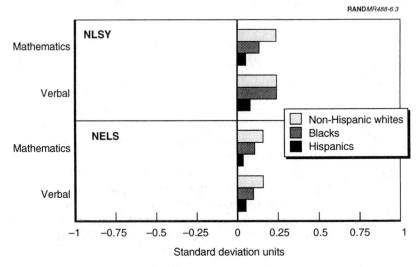

Figure 6.3—Change in Predicted Mean Test Scores by Race/Ethnicity Using Nonpooled Regressions, 1975–1990

The much smaller Hispanic gains, estimated by our equations, can be understood by looking at the changing characteristics of Hispanic families shown in Table 6.4.[6] Because of the influx of new immigrants, most of whom are somewhat less educated and less skilled than previous immigrants, Hispanic families do not exhibit the large gains in parental education that black families do over this time period. In addition, income declined in real terms by about 12 percent, and the proportion of young mothers also increased by over 40 percent. On net, these changes in family characteristics would have a marginally positive effect on test scores but much smaller than those for black and non-Hispanic white families.

Table 6.4

Selected Family Characteristics of Hispanic 15–18-Year-Olds, 1975–1990

Variable	1975	1980	1990	% Change (1975–1990)
Income ($1987)	29,750	30,405	26,073	–12
Mother's education				
Less than high school	63.9	60.5	54.6	–15
High school	26.4	27.2	29.8	+13
Some college	5.7	7.7	10.9	+91
College graduate	3.9	4.5	4.6	+18
Father's education				
Less than high school	61.9	58.7	55.3	–11
High school	22.0	24.4	25.6	+16
Some college	8.3	9.9	12.2	+47
College graduate	7.8	7.1	6.9	–12
Number of siblings				
0–1	39.5	43.7	54.3	+37
2–3	34.2	36.7	37.3	+09
4 or more	26.3	19.6	8.5	–68
Age of mother at child's birth				
≤19 years	11.7	12.3	16.7	+43
20–24 years	29.4	32.9	34.4	+17
25–29 years	29.5	27.6	27.6	–06
≥30 years	29.4	27.2	21.3	–28
Single mother	23.9	21.6	32.1	+34
Mother working	38.9	46.3	55.0	+41

[6]Again, as before, we show the changes in family characteristics for Hispanic youth aged 14–15-years-old in Table B.3. The trends are very similar for the two groups.

SUMMARY

The regression coefficients presented in the last subsection were used to predict mathematics and verbal/reading test scores for samples of children from the Current Population Surveys for selected years. We then computed the mean for each of these predicted test score distributions. The change in the means of the predicted test scores represents our estimate of the effect of changing family and demographic characteristics on test scores over the relevant time period.

We find, overall, that we would predict a *gain* in average test scores from 1970–1990 of about 0.20 of a standard deviation for both mathematics and verbal/reading tests. This is largely due to net positive changes in the family environment over this time period, predominantly the significant increase in parental educational attainment and the substantial decline in family size. Our pooled regression predictions show much larger gains for blacks than for nonblacks because of the larger positive changes experienced by black families. The nonpooled regression predictions (that are based on the separate race/ethnicity models) reveal a somewhat different pattern, with non-Hispanic whites showing larger gains or similar gains to those predicted for blacks. Hispanics are predicted to have the smallest net gains of the three groups, primarily because of the influx of new immigrants, most of whom are less educated and less skilled than previous immigrants. Thus, Hispanics do not exhibit the large positive gains in parental educational attainment and family size experienced by other groups during this time period and, in addition, suffered a decline in real income that further reduced the expected gain in achievement.

For at least two reasons, the results of the analysis remain convincing despite the simplicity of the linear models and the potential bias in the single-parent and working-mother variables. First, when more complex models that contain nonlinear and a full range of interactions terms are used to estimate family effects from 1970/1975 to 1990, there are almost no differences in the average predictions from these models when compared to the simple linear ones. However, we are investigating whether the predictions for youth in multiple-risk situations change using the complex models.

Second, sensitivity analysis shows that our estimates of family effects are relatively insensitive to fairly large changes in the size of the working-mother and single-parent family coefficients. For instance, it would take a coefficient of approximately one standard deviation for single parent to move our family effects by 0.10 of a standard deviation. Even for black families, it would take a coefficient of approximately 0.60 of a standard deviation to change the family effect by 0.10 of a standard deviation. Coefficients of this magnitude are far outside the range of any empirical measurements, and even simple linear models are highly unlikely to have this degree of bias.

Chapter Seven

COMPARING TEST SCORE PREDICTIONS WITH NAEP TRENDS

This chapter compares our predicted test score changes based on changes in family and demographic characteristics to actual changes reported for the National Assessment of Educational Progress tests given to nationally representative samples of the student population at ages 9, 13, and 17 and presents the residual differences that need to be explained by factors other than changing family characteristics. NAEP trend data on 13-year-olds are compared with the predicted trends reported above for the 14–15-year-old NELS sample, and the 17-year-old NAEP scores are compared with the predicted scores for the 15–18-year-old NLSY sample. Several comparisons spanning different time periods are made to see if a broadly consistent pattern emerges. NAEP tests were administered approximately every four years; comparable reading tests were given in 1971, 1975, 1980, and 1990, and comparable mathematics tests were given in 1973, 1978, 1982, and 1990. The 1975 reading tests and the 1978 mathematics tests were the first to identify Hispanics as a separate group (U.S. Department of Education, 1991).

COMPARING NAEP DIFFERENCES AND FAMILY/ DEMOGRAPHIC EFFECTS

We look first at trends in the overall population and for two racial groups—black and nonblack. This allows us to examine trends over the longer time period—between 1970 and 1990. We then compare our predicted trends for the three racial/ethnic groups to 1975–1990 reading NAEP changes and 1978–1990 mathematics NAEP changes.

Pooled Sample of All Races

Figures 7.1 and 7.2 compare the changes in mathematics and verbal/reading NAEP scores for two time periods for 13- and 17-year-old students to the changes predicted based on changing family characteristics and demographics. For mathematics, family/demographic effects would predict gains that differ from actual gains by at most 0.15 of a standard deviation (1973–1990 comparison for 17-year-old students) but differ from actual gains by less than 0.08 of a standard deviation for the other comparisons. The data show that mathematics scores must have declined by less than 0.10 of a standard deviation between 1973 and 1978, since 1973–1990 NAEP differences are smaller than 1978–1990 NAEP differences. This is consistent with the fact that family/demographic changes would predict gains in this time period, since other factors are also operating to change scores.[1]

The reading tests show that NAEP score changes were always less than estimated family/demographic effects for both age groups for both time period comparisons. The differences are approximately 0.10 of a standard deviation. The results indicate that actual scores did not change as much as predicted by family/demographic effects. To determine the extent to which the results are different by racial/ethnic group, we first present the results for black and nonblack groups for the longer time spans, then the 1975–1990 (verbal) and 1978–1990 (mathematics) comparisons for blacks, Hispanics, and non-Hispanic whites.

Pooled Sample of Blacks and Nonblacks

Figures 7.3 and 7.4 compare black and nonblack NAEP scores with estimated family effects for 13- and 17-year-olds for 1971–1990 (verbal/reading) and mathematics (1973–1990). Black students of

---

[1]Comparisons between two time periods must be done with some caution, especially if there are large variations in test scores for one or more years that do not reflect a general trend. As Figure 7.1 illustrates, there could be some sensitivity of results in the range of ±0.10 of a standard deviation, depending on whether comparisons are made using 1973 or 1978 as a starting point. We have made comparisons using all years in the 1970s when NAEP scores are available, and we find that the major conclusions of the report are insensitive to the initial year. At the same time, we have not emphasized those conclusions that are sensitive to such variation.

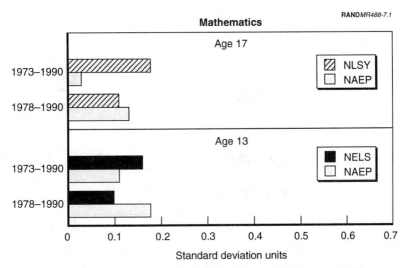

Figure 7.1—Predicted Mean Differences and Actual NAEP Score Differences for Two Periods, Mathematics (1973–1990) and Mathematics (1978–1990)

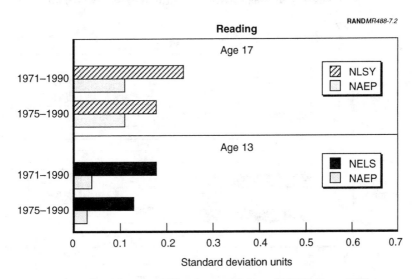

Figure 7.2—Predicted Mean Differences and Actual NAEP Score Differences for Two Periods, Reading (1971–1990) and Reading (1975–1990)

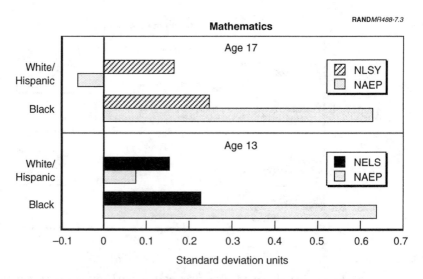

Figure 7.3—Predicted Mean Differences and Actual NAEP Score Differences
for Black and Nonblack Groups, Mathematics (1973–1990)

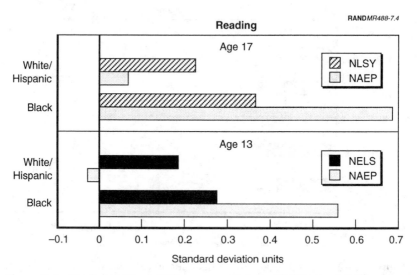

Figure 7.4—Predicted Mean Differences and Actual NAEP Score Differences
for Black and Nonblack Groups, Reading (1971–1990)

both ages have made dramatic gains in both reading and mathematics scores between the early 1970s and 1990. Black scores have increased between 0.50 and 0.70 of a standard deviation in this time period, whereas scores for nonblacks have either declined slightly (0.05 of a standard deviation) or increased slightly. Moreover, changes based on estimated family effects for blacks account for less than one-half of the total gain. The remaining part of the gain presumably might be accounted for by factors outside the family.

The nonblack comparisons show that family effects were always larger than the actual NAEP gains. However, one cause of this may be the expanding Hispanic population that is included in the nonblack sample but cannot be separately identified for this time period. Separating out the Hispanic population will allow us to determine if the Hispanic gains match the black gains and the extent to which the nonblack results are influenced by the Hispanic population. The 1975–1990 and 1978–1990 comparisons that separate the three racial/ethnic groups are discussed in the next subsection.

Comparing Black, Hispanic, and Non-Hispanic White Results

Recall that we developed two sets of achievement equations: first, by including a set of dummy variables to control for race/ethnicity in the model fit to the pooled sample; second, by fitting separate regressions to each of the three racial/ethnic groups. We showed that there was very little difference in predictions based on the two sets of models. Here, we show both sets of predictions in the figures below; they are labeled "pooled estimates" and "nonpooled estimates," respectively.

Math Results. Figures 7.5 and 7.6 show the results for mathematics. The mathematics results are fairly similar for both age groups. The NAEP results show large gains for both minority groups and small gains for non-Hispanic white students. However, family effects can explain less than one-third of the substantial gains for minority students. Family estimates for non-Hispanic whites, on the other hand, are very close to the actual gains made.

Reading Results. Figures 7.7 and 7.8 present the results for reading between 1975 and 1990 for 13- and 17-year-olds for the three racial/ethnic groups. The NAEP scores indicate that 17-year-old blacks and

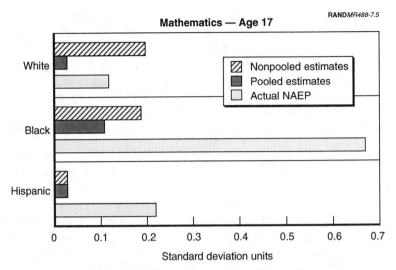

Figure 7.5—Predicted Mean Differences and Actual NAEP Score Differences
for 17-Year-Old Black, Hispanic, and Non-Hispanic White Groups,
Mathematics (1975–1990)

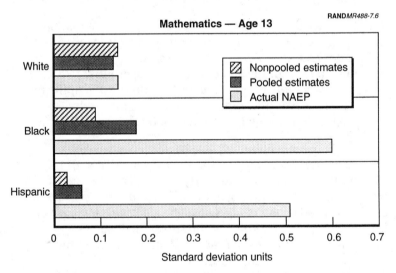

Figure 7.6—Predicted Mean Differences and Actual NAEP Score Differences
for 13-Year-Old Black, Hispanic, and Non-Hispanic White Groups,
Mathematics (1975–1990)

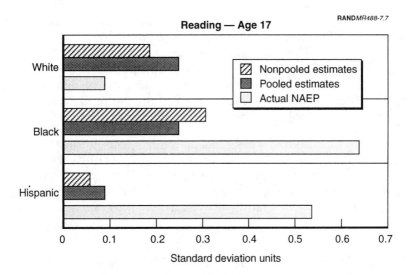

Figure 7.7—Predicted Mean Differences and Actual NAEP Score Differences
for 17-Year-Old Black, Hispanic, and Non-Hispanic White Groups,
Reading (1975–1990)

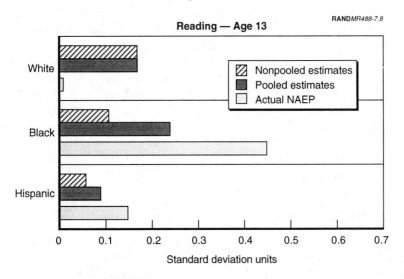

Figure 7.8—Predicted Mean Differences and Actual NAEP Score Differences
for 13-Year-Old Black, Hispanic, and Non-Hispanic White Groups,
Reading (1975–1990)

Hispanics had large gains of over 0.50 of a standard deviation, whereas white scores increased by about 0.10 of a standard deviation. Family effects apparently can account for less than one-half of the black gains and a much smaller proportion of the Hispanic gains. White NAEP gains are somewhat smaller than estimated from family effects for reading. The differences are not particularly sensitive to whether pooled or nonpooled estimates are used.

Thirteen-year-olds show a similar pattern by race/ethnicity (Figure 7.8), but the NAEP gains for all groups are significantly smaller than for 17-year-old youth—especially among the Hispanic students. The non-Hispanic white group again shows a smaller NAEP gain than would be predicted by family effects by over 0.10 of a standard deviation.

THE PATTERN OF RESIDUAL DIFFERENCES BETWEEN NAEP SCORES AND FAMILY EFFECTS

Residual Differences

Figures 7.9 and 7.10 show the residual differences between the actual NAEP scores and our estimates of family effects for mathematics and reading/verbal scores for 13- and 17-year-old youth for each racial/ethnic group and the total population. The mathematics results show large residual gains for black and Hispanic students of between 0.20 and 0.50 of a standard deviation and no residual gain for non-Hispanic white students. The verbal results show somewhat smaller residual gains for minority students, ranging from approximately 0.10 to 0.40 of a standard deviation, but show residual losses of between 0.10 and 0.15 of a standard deviation for non-Hispanic white students.

Interpreting the Results

Hypotheses accounting for the residuals must meet four criteria. First, the hypothesized cause must either be empirically linked to test scores or at least be plausibly linked to having an influence on test scores. Second, the factor must have changed significantly for students over this time period. Third, there must be an explanation for

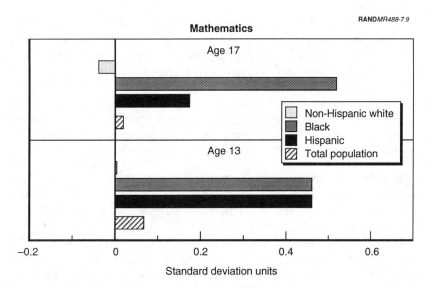

Figure 7.9—Residual Differences Between NAEP and Family Effects on
Mathematics Test Scores for Different Racial/Ethnic Groups, 1978–1990

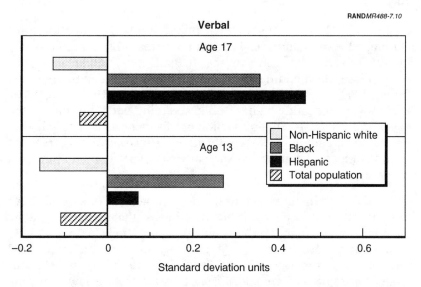

Figure 7.10—Residual Differences Between NAEP and Family Effects on
Verbal Test Scores for Different Racial/Ethnic Groups, 1975–1990

why the factor differentially affected minority scores. Fourth, the factor must not be accounted for by changing family characteristics. Probably the most plausible candidates for explaining this effect are some combination of increased public investment in education and social programs and changed social policies aimed at equalizing educational opportunities—such as school desegregation, bilingual programs, and programs that increased the opportunity of minorities for college admission and jobs. These programs were certainly designed to encourage and produce higher student achievement.

Since these programs were primarily implemented in the late 1960s and during the 1970s and continued through the 1980s, although at a reduced growth rate, they would be expected to primarily affect children born and schooled in the 1970s and 1980s. Our comparisons are between children who were either 13 or 17 between 1970 and 1975 and children who were 13 or 17 in 1990. The first group would have been born in the early 1950s to the early 1960s and been raised and schooled primarily in the late 1950s and 1960s. So the comparison would be between schools and social policies of the late 1950s and 1960s compared to those of the early 1970s through the 1980s.

Fuchs and Reklis (1992) show that public spending on children including education and social programs increased substantially during this period. They estimate that federal, state, and local government per capita spending (in $1988) on children under 18 increased from $1300 in 1960 to $2900 in 1988. Thus, in the 1970s and 1980s, there was significantly higher public spending per child than in the 1950s and 1960s. The major portion of this increase is simply higher per capita spending on K–12 education. However, the figures also include other social programs such as Head Start, food and nutrition programs, and others.

Although it is difficult to determine how these additional funds have been targeted, it is plausible to hypothesize that increased public spending and changing public policies differentially benefitted low-income or minority students. Some programs, such as Title I, food and nutrition programs, Head Start, and bilingual and second-language programs were specifically targeted toward lower-income or minority children. If so, minority scores would be expected to rise more than nonminority scores, since a much greater proportion of minority families would be eligible for the programs.

However, much of the increased spending for children was from large increases made in general K–12 school spending. It is difficult to determine how this general allocation would benefit different kinds of youth. Some additional state funds may have been targeted toward schools or school districts with lower-income or minority students. However, even with increased funding dispersed widely across schools and school districts, it is plausible that a higher proportion of resources was directed toward low-scoring youth in each school or school district.

Desegregation also may have been an important factor, particularly for black students. Desegregation of schools moved a substantial proportion of black students into different schools that may have been better funded and more competitive. Since desegregation occurred primarily in the late 1960s and 1970s, the two comparison groups of black students in our analysis would have probably been schooled in very different environments.

Another factor that requires further investigation is changes in student motivation, brought about by a changing job market and higher college admissions criteria. Although the job market for young workers has deteriorated from 1970 to 1990, especially for high school graduates, with a significant decline in entry-level wages, job and college opportunities for minorities may have improved relative to those for nonminority youth.

The lack of a residual (mathematics) or a negative residual (verbal/reading) for non-Hispanic whites lends itself to several possible interpretations that can be addressed with further research. One interpretation is that family effects for nonminorities are actually smaller than we have estimated with our linear models because marginal differences in income, family size, and parental education affect higher-scoring youth less than lower-scoring youth.[2]

---

[2]We have run fully interactive models with squared terms and used these for estimating family effects. Although the more complex models generally make only very small changes (less than 0.02 of a standard deviation) in the estimated size of the

A second hypothesis is that public spending and changed public policies simply did not benefit non-Hispanic whites. This might be because the most effective policies and programs were those directed primarily toward racial/ethnic groups (desegregation, affirmative action, bilingual programs, etc.). An alternative explanation is that programs that were targeted toward lower-scoring students including all racial groups were less effective for non-Hispanic white students. It should be noted that lower-scoring non-Hispanic white students are much more often located in rural areas than are lower-scoring minority youth. It might be that less attention was given to lower-scoring rural youth or that it is just more difficult to help them because of their dispersion and isolation.

A third explanation is that lower-scoring whites benefited from public investment but there were more than offsetting losses from higher-scoring white youth. Higher-scoring white youth may not have gained as much ground as called for by family effects because of factors independent of public investment and policies. For instance, some have suggested a weakening of the curriculum for higher achieving youth (Rock, 1987). There may also have been an implicit tradeoff in producing the large gains for minority or lower-scoring youth. For example, successfully addressing lower-scoring youth may have resulted in less emphasis and fewer resources for higher-scoring students. These are all important questions that can be explored through future research.

Finally, the results imply that some factors may explain the residuals that are different for mathematics and reading/verbal achievement. One possibility is implementation of a new curriculum for mathematics that was more effective than the new curriculum for reading/verbal skills. Another possibility is differential effects on mathematics/verbal skills from factors outside the school. Since reading/verbal skills are probably more influenced by factors outside school, and mathematics is probably more influenced by within-school factors, there may have been differential effects from higher

---

family effects, it should be noted that the largest change is for non-Hispanic white students for reading/verbal scores when the results show a decline in family effect of 0.05 of a standard deviation. This reduces the size of the negative residual somewhat for non-Hispanic white students.

school investments or changes in the nonfamily external environment.

SUMMARY

The comparisons between NAEP differences and estimated family/demographic effects show that the large minority NAEP gains by both 13- and 17-year-old black and Hispanic students cannot be accounted for by changing family characteristics alone. On the other hand, the gains made by non-Hispanic white students can be accounted for almost entirely by changes in the family. In fact, actual gains by non-Hispanic white students in verbal/reading scores are lower than would be predicted by family effects.

We discuss the pattern of these residuals to attempt to identify factors that might explain the large residuals for minorities and the lack of residual gains by majority students. The pattern is certainly consistent with the effects that might be expected from changing public policies directed at providing equal educational opportunity and increased level of public investment. However, further research is necessary to better identify the specific factors that might account for the pattern of residuals.

Chapter Eight

CONCLUSIONS AND FUTURE RESEARCH

CONCLUSIONS

The primary objectives of this study were to analyze the trends in mathematics and verbal/reading achievement scores in the period 1970/75 to 1990 to:

- Assess the net effect of changing family and demographic characteristics on test score trends between 1970/75 and 1990.

- Compare these family/demographic effects to actual changes in scores to determine whether other factors are needed to explain score trends.

- Develop hypotheses that would help explain the pattern of residual effects; some likely candidates are changing public policies and increased public investment and changes in the quality and productivity of schools.

In terms of student achievement, our estimates do not support the commonly held perception that the American family environment has deteriorated. Test scores of 14–18-year-old youth would have risen about 0.20 of a standard deviation from the combined effect of changes that have occurred in family and demographic characteristics between 1970 and 1990. The most significant family characteristics associated with test scores are parental education levels, family income, family size, and age of mother at child's birth. Other things equal, higher levels of parental education and family income are associated with significantly higher test scores. Smaller family size and older mothers also are associated with higher test scores. The presence of a working mother at child's age of 14 is associated with small gains in test scores, whereas the variable measuring single-parent household—other things equal—has no association with test scores.

For three reasons, our results differ from the "conventional wisdom" that the family environment for children has deteriorated over the last 20 years. First, two highly significant—but often overlooked—changes in family characteristics have had positive effects on test scores: the very large increase in parental education levels and the significant reduction in family size.

Second, factors that are popularly associated with a deterioration of the family environment—increasing numbers of single-parent households and children with working mothers—have much smaller effects on test scores—other things equal—than family size and parental education level.

Third, although family income is strongly associated with test scores, the average family income has not changed significantly over the 1970 to 1990 period for families of eighth graders or 15–18-year-old children.

The predicted positive family effects on test scores are largest and nearly equal for blacks and non-Hispanic whites, but much smaller for Hispanic youth. Although both black and non-Hispanic white families registered large gains in parental education, reduced family size, and stable real family income, Hispanic families showed much smaller gains in parents' educational attainment, smaller reductions in family size, and declines in family income. These differences are probably due to the continuing large immigration of Hispanic families with lower levels of education and income into the country.

National mathematics and verbal/reading test scores of representative samples of U.S. students aged 13 and 17 have risen over the last 20 years by about the same magnitude, or slightly less than the estimated family/demographic effects. However, the NAEP scores disaggregated by racial/ethnic group show very strong gains for black and Hispanic students, and small gains or losses for non-Hispanic white youth. Comparisons of our estimated gains by racial/ethnic group show that the actual gain in black and Hispanic scores far exceeds the gain predicted from family characteristics alone. Family gains account for approximately one-third of the minority gains. For non-Hispanic whites, the actual mathematics gains are approximately equal to family gains, but family gains slightly exceed actual gains in verbal scores.

The most likely explanation for the gains made by black and Hispanic students over and above those predicted by family effects is changes in public policies and the very large increases in public investment in social and educational programs aimed at minorities and lower-achieving students. Further research is needed to better identify those programs and policies that were effective.

The lack of residual gains for non-Hispanic white students also needs further research. First, programs designed to aid all lower-income or lower-scoring youth may not have been effective for non-Hispanic white students. For example, a greater proportion of lower-scoring/low-income non-Hispanic white youth came from rural areas, and the increased dispersion and the absence of economies of scale in such areas may have made these programs less effective. Second, these programs may have had an effect on lower-scoring/lower-income non-Hispanic white students but at the expense of offsetting declines among higher-scoring students. For instance, it is possible that a resource tradeoff existed between low- and high-scoring students that reduced the resources and scores of higher-scoring students while allocating more resources to lower-scoring students, resulting in large test score gains.

Our results also suggest that schools attended by 14–18-year-olds in 1990 are roughly equivalent to those attended by youth in 1970, when considering mathematics and reading/verbal instruction. If we assume that constant resources were devoted to mathematics and verbal/reading skills, then our results suggest that there were little or no educational productivity gains as measured by mathematics and verbal/reading test score trends. However, to fully assess changes in school quality and productivity, further work needs to account for changes in curriculum, instruction, school climate, and instructional resources.

When comparing estimated family effects with NAEP scores for the younger NELS sample and for periods from the late 1970s or early 1980s to 1990, the NAEP gains and estimated family effects shrink in size, although both remain positive. This might indicate that the positive effects stemming from changing family characteristics are becoming smaller for younger cohorts during the 1980s. Further research is being done to see how estimated family effects might differ for younger children.

FUTURE RESEARCH

What Additional Factors Account for Minority Gains in Test Scores?

Two important questions that we will address in future work are: (a) What has caused the large gains in minority scores over and above those stemming from changing family characteristics? and (b) Have lower-scoring nonminority youth also experienced similar gains? These questions are critical to establishing future directions for American schools. We are currently conducting research along several lines that will help provide answers to these and related questions.

The multiple-risk hypothesis. The child development and more clinically oriented literature focuses on the effects of multiple-risk factors on children. The underlying hypothesis implies that test scores might fall dramatically (nonlinearly or exponentially) when children are under conditions of multiple risk. Basically, this means that the effects on test scores of having low family income and low levels of parental education are worse than the additive effects of each factor independently. One can regard this as a sort of a slippery slope where student achievement falls drastically with every new risk added to the child's life. However, as risks decline, student achievement should go up dramatically as well. Models incorporating the multiple-risk concept may help explain the rapid gains in the test scores of minority students.

Our analysis shows that the primary cognitive family risks include being born to a teenage mother, being in a low-income household, having parents with low educational attainment, and being in a large family. We are currently developing more sophisticated models that incorporate the concept of multiple risk.

Changes in school environment. Our analysis is limited to the effects of family factors on student achievement. However, if changes in school characteristics are associated with improved scores, and if the school environment facing minorities, particularly blacks, has improved over time, then this may help explain the large minority gains in achievement. Some evidence exists to show that school characteristics do affect test scores of minorities. Moreover, the school environment for black children certainly changed dramatically over the past 20 years, with increased desegregation, net migration from the south, and increased spending on education. These changes may have produced better school environments and may have helped foster the academic achievement gains.

Other factors. Another possible explanation for minority test score gains may be changes in student motivation. There is evidence to suggest that the proximal home environment—in terms of emphasis on learning, amount of time spent on homework, and high parental expectations—can significantly affect student achievement. The key question is whether there were differential changes in minority student motivation occurring during this time period. Although this is a difficult question to answer because student motivation is difficult to quantify, we can suggest some factors that may have had a favorable effect on minority student motivation. For example, blacks began to have access to better and more competitive classrooms as a result of integration, there were increased opportunities for college for both children and parents, and this undoubtedly led to higher parental expectations for children's achievement. In addition, the economic literature suggests that, at this time, blacks faced increased returns to education compared to whites; this may have increased expectations and the desire to stay in and do well in school.

Developing Better Indicators of At-Risk Children

Several federal and state policies are directed toward at-risk children. These policies use a variety of measures to define at-risk populations but usually depend on one or two measures with somewhat arbitrary cutoffs. Many additional risk factors (other than those incorporated in the family models) need to be identified. Models based on more inclusive cognitive risk factors can help provide a better basis for identifying populations of at-risk children and for estimating changes in the size and location of these populations. In the longer run, we need to develop a framework that allows comparisons of the incidence of risk, the populations at risk, the effectiveness of programs to alleviate risks, and the costs of such programs. Such analyses need to be done for different populations of at-risk children, since there will be differences across risks and types of children in what is effective.

Effects on Younger Children

Our analysis focuses on changes in families with children between the ages of 14 and 18 between 1970 and 1990. Some believe that the family environment may have worsened for younger children, particularly during the last ten years, so if we duplicated our analysis for 14–18-year-olds in the year 2000, our results may be different. To test this hypothesis, our methodology can be used to study younger children and more recent trends.

DERIVING SHIFTS IN TEST SCORES FROM CHANGING FAMILY CHARACTERISTICS AND DEMOGRAPHIC COMPOSITION

Under ideal conditions, datasets would be available at two times for representative groups of similarly aged youth that contain both test scores and the important variables that determine test scores. If we have two representative samples of students at time t_1 and t_2, then test scores are given by:

$$T_i^{t1} = a^{t1} + \sum_n b_n^{t1} X_{n_i}^{t1} + \sum_m c_m^{t1} Y_{m_i}^{t1} \tag{1}$$

$$T_j^{t2} = a^{t2} + \sum_n b_n^{t2} X_{n_j}^{t2} + \sum_m c_m^{t2} Y_{m_j}^{t2} \tag{2}$$

where

T_i^t = test score for student i at time t,

$X_{n_i}^t$ = family characteristics and demographic variables for student i at time t,

$Y_{m_j}^t$ = school, community, and other nonfamily variables for student j at time t,

a^t, b_n^t, c_m^t = linear regression coefficients.

The shift in the mean test score can be estimated as:

$$\Delta T = \overline{T}^{t2} - \overline{T}^{t1} = \Delta a + \sum_n (\Delta X_n \overline{b}_n + \overline{X}_n \Delta b_n) + \sum_m (\Delta Y_m \overline{c}_m + \overline{Y}_m \Delta c_m)$$

where

$\Delta \overline{X}_n = \overline{X}_n^{t2} - \overline{X}_n^{t1}$ = shift in family or demographic characteristics,

$\Delta \overline{Y}_m = \overline{Y}_m^{t2} - Y_m^{t1}$ = shift in nonfamily characteristics,

$\overline{b}_n = \dfrac{b_n^{t2} + b_n^{t1}}{2}$ = average of family coefficients,

$\overline{c}_m = \dfrac{c_m^{t2} + c_m^{t1}}{2}$ = average of nonfamily coefficients,

$\Delta b_n = b_n^{t2} - b_n^{t1}$ = change in family coefficients,

$\Delta c_m = c_m^{t2} - c_m^{t1}$ = change in nonfamily coefficients.

The first term is the shift in the intercept term that is unrelated to changes in family or demographic composition. The second term is the estimated mean shift in test scores resulting from changes in family characteristics and demographic composition. The third term accounts for shifts in nonfamily variables. We are trying to estimate only the shift resulting from family and demographic composition. This is given by:

$$\Delta T_{\text{fam}} = \sum_n (\Delta X_n \overline{b}_n + \overline{X}_n \Delta b_n)$$

Since we estimate only the equations with the family and demographic variables, we, of course, assume that the coefficients of family and demographic variables are independent of, and not biased by, the exclusion of the other variables from our equations.[1]

---

[1] We have done further estimation with the NELS sample, which includes variables corresponding to school, community, and parenting variables, and the changes in the basic family and demographic coefficients are very small compared to the coefficient itself.

There are two terms in this equation. The first corresponds to the direct shift resulting from changes in family and demographic composition, holding the coefficients constant. The second term represents the effect of structural shifts in coefficients, holding family and demographic composition constant. For instance, the effect of family income on test scores may shift over time. These structural shifts can be caused by cultural and policy changes affecting families but not by simple changes in family and demographic composition, assuming linearity.

Since we do not have samples of similarly aged children at two times, we cannot estimate with our data the structural shifts in coefficients. The structural coefficients would be expected to be functions of the age of the children, so the difference in coefficients we find between the NELS and NLSY cannot be attributed only to structural shifts in coefficients.

In our estimates we thus treat the NELS and NLSY estimates as simply independent estimates of the mean structural coefficient for each age group and make estimates of mean shifts in test scores for each age group, using the NLSY and NELS equations. Assuming that no structural shifts in coefficients have occurred over the 1970–1990 time period of our measurements, our results will accurately measure the effect of family and demographic composition shifts.

If shifts in coefficients are occurring, the bias in our measurements will be small if:

$$\sum_n \bar{X}_n \Delta b_n < \sum_n \bar{b} \Delta X_n$$

If changes in coefficients simply reflect offsetting shifts among coefficients, bias from changes might be small even though large shifts occur in individual coefficients. For instance, we find that the NELS results have stronger education effects but weaker income effects compared to those of the NLSY. Such shifts can be partially offsetting.

PROFILE OF FAMILIES OF 14–15-YEAR-OLD YOUTH

Table B.1

Profile of 14–15-Year-Olds, 1970–1990

Variable	1970	1980	1990	% Change (1970– 1990)
Income ($1987)	36,645	37,837	37,105	+1
Mother's education				
Less than high school	38.3	27.0	17.3	−55
High school	44.9	45.6	45.4	+1
Some college	10.2	16.0	21.4	+110
College graduate	6.6	11.4	16.0	+142
Father's education				
Less than high school	42.8	29.8	18.9	−56
High school	33.3	35.6	37.4	+12
Some college	10.9	15.7	20.8	+91
College graduate	13.1	18.9	22.9	+75
Number of siblings				
0–1	39.1	52.0	64.8	+66
2–3	38.5	37.8	30.1	−22
4 or more	22.3	10.2	5.1	−77
Age of mother at child's birth				
≤19 years	9.2	10.6	14.4	+56
20–24 years	29.0	32.0	32.1	+11
25–29 years	30.2	30.0	32.9	+9
≥30 years	31.5	27.4	20.7	+34
Single mother	13.8	19.8	23.1	+67
Mother working	47.7	58.3	68.5	+44
Race				
Black	12.6	13.9	14.6	+16
Nonblack	87.4	86.1	85.4	−0.02

Table B.2

Profile of Black and Nonblack 14–15-Year-Olds, 1970–1990

	Black				Nonblack			
Variable	1970	1980	1990	% Change	1970	1980	1990	% Change (1970– 1990)
Income ($1987)	22,436	22,272	23,668	+5	38,702	40,355	39,401	+2
Mother's education								
Less than high school	63.8	44.0	22.4	−65	34.6	24.3	16.4	−53
High school	29.3	39.3	50.0	+71	47.2	46.6	44.6	−6
Some college	4.2	12.2	18.9	+350	11.0	16.7	21.8	+98
College graduate	2.7	4.5	8.7	+222	7.2	12.5	17.2	+139
Father's education								
Less than high school	70.3	51.8	25.0	−64	38.8	26.2	17.9	+54
High school	22.8	33.3	48.5	+113	34.8	36.0	35.5	+2
Some college	3.7	11.7	16.8	+354	11.9	16.3	21.5	+81
College graduate	3.3	3.1	9.7	+194	14.5	21.5	25.1	+73
Number of siblings								
0–1	27.4	41.4	56.7	+107	40.8	53.7	66.2	+62
2–3	34.1	36.2	33.9	−1	39.1	38.1	29.5	−25
4 or more	38.5	22.4	9.4	−76	20.0	8.2	4.3	−79
Age of mother at child's birth								
≤19 years	14.3	19.6	29.3	+105	8.5	9.1	11.8	+39
20–24 years	27.5	29.1	32.5	+18	29.2	32.4	32.0	+10
25–29 years	26.6	25.8	19.8	−26	30.7	30.7	35.1	+14
≥30 years	31.6	25.4	18.4	−42	31.5	27.7	21.0	−33
Single mother	36.9	48.4	50.5	+37	10.4	15.1	18.5	+78
Mother working	52.2	55.4	69.0	+32	47.0	58.8	68.4	+46

Table B.3

Profile of Hispanic 14–15-Year-Olds, 1975–1990

Variable	1975	1980	1990	% Change (1975– 1990)
Income ($1987)	26,194	29,927	26,024	+0
Mother's education				
Less than high school	68.2	55.9	51.9	−24
High school	22.4	29.2	32.8	+46
Some college	5.6	9.1	10.9	+95
College graduate	3.8	5.8	14.5	+18
Father's education				
Less than high school	59.4	56.4	54.5	−8
High school	24.7	26.1	26.4	+7
Some college	9.0	8.9	11.2	+24
College graduate	6.9	8.6	7.9	+14
Number of siblings				
0–1	28.1	39.3	46.8	+67
2–3	41.5	40.6	42.1	+1
4 or more	30.3	20.0	11.1	−63
Age of mother at child's birth				
≤19 years	13.7	14.7	18.8	+37
20–24 years	29.1	28.5	36.3	+25
25–29 years	29.1	31.6	24.7	−15
≥30 years	28.2	25.2	20.2	−28
Single mother	26.3	21.4	30.0	+14
Mother working	37.3	47.6	54.0	+45

WEIGHTED AND UNWEIGHTED REGRESSION RESULTS

Table C.1
Weighted and Unweighted Regression Results, Mathematics and Verbal, NLSY

Variable	Mathematics				Verbal			
	Unweighted		Weighted		Unweighted		Weighted	
	Coef.	t-Stat.	Coef.	t-Stat.	Coef.	t-Stat.	Coef.	t-Stat.
Intercept	-0.541	-8.393	-0.447	-6.995	-0.533	-8.302	-0.335	-5.497
Income	0.0075	10.479	0.0063	9.688	0.0071	9.979	0.0052	8.526
Mother's education								
Less than high school	-0.167	-5.391	-0.166	-5.401	-0.255	-8.307	-0.256	-8.743
Some college	0.145	3.081	0.133	3.212	0.143	3.051	0.086	2.183
College graduate	0.150	2.694	0.126	2.724	0.177	3.178	0.160	3.635
Father's education								
Less than high school	-0.190	-6.11	-0.193	-6.289	-0.214	-6.916	-0.185	-6.337
Some college	0.163	3.451	0.118	2.821	0.208	4.412	0.196	4.913
College graduate	0.326	6.961	0.329	8.335	0.362	7.776	0.375	9.966
Age of mother at child's birth	0.011	5.830	0.011	5.948	0.016	8.550	0.014	7.460
Number of siblings	-0.043	-8.402	-0.046	-8.026	-0.071	-13.701	-0.062	-11.370
Single mother	-0.010	-0.297	-0.020	-0.554	-0.0043	-0.134	0.004	0.125
Mother working	0.075	3.085	0.091	3.818	0.089	3.655	0.066	2.899
Female	0.165	6.983	0.159	6.863	0.139	5.917	0.130	5.906
Black	-0.488	-15.796	-0.581	-15.449	-0.546	-17.733	-0.664	-18.537
Hispanic	-0.159	-4.116	-0.283	-5.170	-0.217	-5.619	-0.350	-6.706
Northeast	0.084	2.471	0.146	4.418	0.134	3.934	0.122	3.857
North Central	0.191	6.052	0.184	6.160	0.143	4.563	0.117	4.094
West	0.025	0.704	0.053	1.442	0.064	1.774	0.076	2.178
Income missing	0.0019	0.059	0.041	1.318	0.016	0.499	0.0003	0.010
Mother's education missing	-0.275	-4.084	-0.347	-4.472	-0.272	-4.049	-0.278	-3.754
Father's education missing	-0.092	-2.198	-0.101	-2.027	-0.124	-2.967	-0.155	-3.260
Age of mother missing	0.047	0.881	-0.012	-0.210	0.056	1.059	-0.032	-0.579

Table C.2
Weighted and Unweighted Regression Results, Mathematics and Reading, NELS

Variable	Mathematics				Reading			
	Unweighted		Weighted		Unweighted		Weighted	
	Coef.	t-Stat.	Coef.	t-Stat.	Coef.	t-Stat.	Coef.	t-Stat.
Intercept	-0.269	-8.418	-0.269	-8.444	-0.310	-9.551	-0.323	-9.949
Income	0.0024	14.991	0.0025	13.003	0.0015	9.347	0.0015	7.833
Mother's education								
Less than high school	-0.147	-7.8	-0.169	-9.190	-0.174	-9.085	-0.201	-10.722
Some college	0.136	8.421	0.115	7.291	0.147	8.973	0.129	7.995
College graduate	0.394	20.058	0.375	18.699	0.346	17.329	0.333	16.278
Father's education								
Less than high school	-0.142	-7.571	-0.144	-7.852	-0.143	-7.464	-0.141	-7.538
Some college	0.156	9.141	0.147	8.764	0.157	9.016	0.150	8.747
College graduate	0.414	22.129	0.378	20.262	0.348	18.298	0.318	16.700
Age of mother at child's birth	0.0069	6.576	0.0058	5.570	0.0079	7.409	0.0076	7.144
Number of siblings	-0.018	-4.505	-0.015	-3.779	-0.037	-9.003	-0.033	-8.030
Single mother	-0.034	1.883	-0.026	-1.429	-0.034	-1.848	-0.028	-1.504
Mother working	-0.0034	-0.273	-0.014	-1.124	0.0033	0.26	-0.003	-0.223
Female	-0.025	-2.188	-0.007	-0.576	0.217	18.508	0.241	20.522
Black	-0.591	-31.522	-0.583	-31.819	-0.508	-26.646	-0.533	-28.477
Hispanic	-0.338	-18.101	-0.319	-15.661	-0.273	-14.432	-0.286	-13.766
Northeast	0.083	5.084	0.090	5.447	0.083	4.979	0.079	4.636
North Central	0.100	6.544	0.126	8.348	0.044	2.864	0.054	3.517
West	0.034	2.059	0.037	2.200	-0.046	-2.73	-0.023	-1.332
Income missing	-0.0026	-0.092	0.0003	0.011	-0.023	-0.773	-0.018	-0.602
Mother's education missing	-0.119	-2.483	-0.208	-3.999	-0.165	-3.392	-0.231	-4.387
Father's education missing	-0.112	-4.336	-0.114	-4.364	-0.132	-5.016	-0.124	-4.663
Number of siblings missing	-0.127	-2.415	-0.154	-2.869	-0.109	-2.041	-0.123	-2.258
Age of mother missing	-0.102	-2.782	-0.133	-3.634	-0.120	-3.212	-0.128	-3.429
Type of household missing	-0.193	-6.008	-0.183	-5.790	-0.125	-3.841	-0.095	-2.941
Mother's work status missing	-0.060	-1.282	-0.042	-0.904	-0.055	-1.148	-0.044	-0.921

BIBLIOGRAPHY

Alwin, Duane F., "Family of Origin and Cohort Differences in Verbal Ability," *American Sociological Review*, Vol. 56, 1991, pp. 625–638.

Armor, David J., "The Fate of Black America: IV. Why Is Black Education Achievement Rising?" *The Public Interest*, 1992, pp. 65–80.

Baily, Martin Neil, "Productivity and the Services of Capital and Labor," in W. C. Brainard and George L. Perry (eds.), *Brookings Papers on Economic Activity*, Vol. 1, 1981, pp. 1–65.

Baumrind, Diana, "Parental Disciplinary Patterns and Social Competence in Children," *Youth and Society*, Vol. 9, 1978, pp. 239–275.

Becker, Gary, *A Treatise on the Family*, Cambridge, Mass.: Harvard University Press, 1981.

Becker, Gary, and Nigel Tomes, "Human Capital and the Rise and Fall of Families," *Journal of Labor Economics*, Vol. 4, 1986, pp. s1–s39.

Bishop, John H., "Is the Test Score Decline Responsible for the Productivity Growth Decline?" *The American Economic Review*, Vol. 79, No. 1, 1989, pp. 178–197.

Blake, Judith, *Family Size and Achievement*, Berkeley, Calif.: University of California Press, 1989.

Blau, Francine D., and Adam J. Grossberg, "Maternal Labor Supply and Children's Cognitive Development," *The Review of Economics and Statistics*, Vol. 74, 1992, pp. 474–481.

Bock, R. Darrell, and Elsie G. J. Moore, *Profile of American Youth: Demographic Influences on ASVAB Test Performance*, Chicago, Ill.: National Opinion Research Center, 1984.

Borjas, George J., *Friends or Strangers: The Impact of Immigrants on the U.S. Economy*, New York, N.Y.: Basic Books, Inc., 1990.

Bradley, R. H., "The Home Inventory: Rationale and Research," in J. Lachenmeyer and M. Gibbs (eds.), *Recent Research in Developmental Psychopathology*, Gardner, N.Y.: Book Supplement to the *Journal of Child Psychology and Psychiatry*, 1985, pp. 191–201.

Caplan, Nathan, Marcella H. Choy, and John K. Whitmore, *Children of the Boat People: A Study of Educational Success*, Ann Arbor, Mich.: The University of Michigan Press, 1991.

Caplan, Nathan, Marcella H. Choy, and John K. Whitmore, "Indochinese Refugee Families and Academic Achievement," *Scientific American*, Vol. 266, No. 2, 1992, pp. 36–42.

Center for Human Resource Research, *NLS Users' Guide, 1992*, Columbus, Ohio: Ohio State University, 1992.

Coleman, James S., Ernest Q. Campbell, Carol J. Hobson, James McPartland, Alexander M. Mood, Frederic D. Weinfeld, and Robert L. York, *Equality of Educational Opportunity*, Washington, D.C.: U.S. Government Printing Office, 1966.

Coleman, James S., and Thomas Hoffer, *Public and Private High Schools: The Impact of Communities*, New York, N.Y.: Basic Books, 1987.

"College Bound Seniors: 1991 Profile of SAT and Achievement Test Takers," Princeton, N.J.: College Entrance Examination Board, 1991.

Demo, David H., "Parent-Child Relations: Assessing Recent Changes," *Journal of Marriage and Family*, Vol. 54, 1992, pp. 104–117.

Demo, David H., and Alan C. Acock, "The Impact of Divorce on Children," *Journal of Marriage and Family*, Vol. 50, 1988, pp. 619–648.

Desai, Sonalde, P. Lindsay Chase-Lansdale, and Robert T. Michael, "Mother or Market? Effects of Maternal Employment on the Intellectual Ability of 4-Year-Old Children," *Demography*, Vol. 26, 1989, pp. 545–561.

Dornbusch, Sanford M., Philip L. Ritter, P. Herbert Leiderman, Donald F. Roberts, and Michael J. Fraleigh, "The Relation of Parenting Style to Adolescent School Performance," *Child Development*, Vol. 58, 1987, pp. 1244–1257.

DuMouchel, William H., and Greg J. Duncan, "Using Sample Survey Weights in Multiple Regression Analyses of Stratified Samples," *Journal of the American Statistical Association*, Vol. 78, No. 383, 1983, pp. 535–543.

Dunn, Judy, and Robert Plomin, *Separate Lives: Why Siblings Are So Different*, New York, N.Y.: Basic Books, Inc., 1990.

Ekstrom, Ruth B., Margaret E. Goertz, Judith M. Pollack, and Donald A. Rock, "Who Drops Out of High School and Why? Findings from a National Study," *Teachers College Record*, Vol. 87, No. 3, 1986, pp. 356–373.

Ensminger, Margaret E., and Anita L. Slusarcick, "Paths to High School Graduation or Dropout: A Longitudinal Study of a First-Grade Cohort," *Sociology of Education*, Vol. 65, 1992, pp. 95–113.

Epstein, Joyce L., "School and Family Connections: Theory, Research, and Implications for Integrating Sociologies of Education and Family," *Marriage and Family Review*, Vol. 15, 1990, pp. 99–126.

Fuchs, Victor R., and Diane M. Reklis, "America's Children: Economic Perspectives and Policy Options," *Science*, Vol. 255, 1992, pp. 41–46.

Gamoran, Adam, "The Stratification of High School Learning Opportunities," *Sociology of Education*, Vol. 60, 1987, pp. 135–155.

Gottfried, Adele Eskeles, Allen W. Gottfried, and Kay Bathhurst, "Maternal Employment, Family Environment, and Children's Development: Infancy Through the School Years," *Maternal Employment and Children's Development: Longitudinal Research*,

Adele E. Gottfried and Allen W. Gottfried (eds.), New York, N.Y.: Plenum Press, 1988.

Grissmer, David W., and Sheila Nataraj Kirby, *Changing Patterns of Nonprior Service Attrition in the Army National Guard and Army Reserve*, Santa Monica, Calif.: RAND, R-3626-RA, 1988.

Hagan, John, "Destiny and Drift: Subcultural Preferences, Status Attainment, and the Risks and Rewards of Youth," *American Sociological Review*, Vol. 56, 1991, pp. 567–582.

Hanushek, Eric A., "The Trade-off Between Child Quantity and Quality," *Journal of Political Economy*, Vol. 100, 1992, pp. 84–117.

Hetherington, E. Mavis, Kathleen Camara, and David L. Featherman, *Cognitive Performances, School Behavior, and Achievement of Children from One-Parent Households*, Washington, D.C.: National Institute of Education, 1981.

Hill, M. Anne, and June O'Neill, "Family Endowment and the Achievement of Young Children with Special Reference to the Underclass," unpublished mimeo, 1993.

Hill, M. Anne, and June O'Neill, "The Transmission of Cognitive Achievement Across Three Generations," working paper, March 1992.

Hoffman, Lois Wladis, "Effects of Maternal Employment in the Two-Parent Family," *American Psychologist*, Vol. 44, 1989, pp. 283–292.

Ingels, Steven J., Sameer Y. Abraham, Rosemary Karr, Bruce D. Spencer, and Martin R. Frankel, "National Education Longitudinal Study of 1988: Data File User's Manual," Washington, D.C.: U.S. Department of Education, National Center for Education Statistics, 1990.

Jencks, C., "Is the American Underclass Growing?" in C. Jencks and P. E. Peterson (eds.), *The Urban Underclass*, Washington, D.C.: The Brookings Institution, 1991, pp. 28–100.

Jencks, Christopher S., Marshall Smith, Henry Acland, Mary Jo Bane, David Cohen, Herbert Gintis, Barbara Hayns, and Stephan

Michelson, "Inequality: A Reassessment of the Effect of Family and Schooling in America," New York, N.Y.: Basic Books, 1972.

Johnson, Eugene G., and Nancy L. Allen, *The NAEP 1990 Technical Report*, Washington, D.C.: National Center for Education Statistics, 1992.

Kaplan, Jay L., and Edward C. Luck, "The Dropout Phenomenon as a Social Problem," *Educational Forum*, Vol. 42, No. 1, November 1977, pp. 41–56.

Kaufman, Phillip, and Kenneth A. Rasinski, "National Education Longitudinal Study of 1988: Quality of the Responses of Eighth-Grade Students in NELS:88," Washington, D.C.: U.S. Department of Education, National Center for Education Statistics, 1991.

Kendrick, John W., "Survey of the Factors Contributing to the Decline in U.S. Productivity Growth," in *The Decline in Productivity Growth*, sponsored by the Federal Reserve Bank of Boston, June 1980.

Kirby, Sheila Nataraj, and David W. Grissmer, *Reassessing Enlisted Reserve Attrition; A Total Force Perspective*, Santa Monica, Calif.: RAND, N-3521-RA, 1993.

Kohn, Melvin L., and Carmi Schooler, *Work and Personality: An Inquiry Into the Impact of Social Stratification*, Ablex Publishing Corporation, 1983.

Koretz, Daniel, *Trends in Educational Achievement*, Washington, D.C.: Congressional Budget Office, 1986.

Koretz, Daniel, *Educational Achievement: Explanations and Implications of Recent Trends*, Washington, D.C.: U.S. Congressional Budget Office, 1987.

Koretz, Daniel, "State Comparisons Using NAEP: Large Costs, Disappointing Benefits," *Educational Researcher*, Vol. 20, 1991, pp. 19–21.

Koretz, Daniel, "What Happened to Test Scores, and Why?" *Educational Measurement: Issues and Practice*, 1992, pp. 7–11.

Krein, Sheila Fitzerald, and Andrea H. Beller, "Educational Attainment of Children from Single-Parent Families: Differences by Exposure, Gender, and Race," *Demography*, Vol. 25, 1988, pp. 221–234.

Kuh, Edwin, "The Validity of Cross-Sectionally Estimated Behavior Equations in Time Series Applications," *Econometrica*, Vol. 27, 1959, pp. 197–214.

Lee, Eun Sul, Ronald N. Forthofer, and Ronald J. Lorimor, *Analyzing Complex Survey Data*, Newbury Park, Calif.: Sara Miller McCune, Sage Publications, Inc., 1990.

Leibowitz, Arleen, "Home Investment in Children," *Journal of Political Economy*, Vol. 82, 1974, pp. s111–s135.

Lindert, Peter H., "Sibling Position and Achievement," *The Journal of Human Resources*, Vol. 12, No. 2, 1977, pp. 198–219.

Linn, Robert L., and Stephen B. Duñbar, "The Nation's Report Card Goes Home: Good News and Bad About Trends in Achievement," *Phi Delta Kappan*, 1990, pp. 127–133.

Marquis, M. Susan, and Sheila Nataraj Kirby, *Economic Factors in Reserve Attrition: Prior Service Individuals in the Army National Guard and Army Reserve*, Santa Monica, Calif.: RAND, R-3686-RA, 1989.

Menaghan, Elizabeth G., and Toby L. Parcel, "Determining Children's Home Environments: The Impact of Maternal Characteristics and Current Occupational and Family Conditions," *Journal of Marriage and the Family*, Vol. 53, 1991, pp. 417–431.

Milne, Ann M., David E. Myers, Alvin Rosenthal, and Alan Ginsburg, "Single Parents, Working Mothers, and the Educational Achievement of School Children," *Sociology of Education*, Vol. 59, 1986, pp. 125–139.

Moore, Kristin A., and Nancy O. Snyder, "Coginitive Achievement Among First-Born Children of Adolescent Mothers," *American Sociological Review*, Vol. 56, October 1991, pp. 612–624.

Murnane, Richard, "Comparisons of Private and Public Schools: What Can We Learn?" in Daniel Levy (ed.), *Private Education: Studies in Choice and Public Policy*, New York, N.Y.: Oxford University Press, 1986, pp. 153–169.

Nisbett, Richard, and Lee Ross, *Human Inference: Strategies and Shortcomings of Social Judgment*, Englewood Cliffs, N.J.: Prentice-Hall, Inc., 1980.

Pallas, A., "The Determinants of High School Dropout," Unpublished Ph.D. dissertation, Baltimore, Md.: Johns Hopkins University, 1984.

Parcel, Toby L., and Elizabeth G. Menaghan, "Maternal Working Conditions and Children's Verbal Facility: Studying the Intergenerational Transmission of Inequality from Mothers to Young Children," *Social Psychology Quarterly*, Vol. 53, 1990, pp. 132–147.

Plomin, Robert, *Development, Genetics, and Psychology*, Hillsdale, N.Y.: Laurence Erlbaum, 1986.

Rasinski, Kenneth A., Steven J. Ingels, Donald A. Rock, and Judith M. Pollack, *America's High School Sophomores: A Ten Year Comparison*, Washington, D.C.: U.S. Department of Education, National Center for Education Statistics, 1993.

Rock, Donald A., "The Score Decline from 1972 to 1980: What Went Wrong?" *Youth and Society*, Vol. 18, No. 3, 1987, pp. 239–254.

Rock, Donald A., and Judith Pollack, *Psychometric Report of the NELS:88 Base Year Test Battery*, Washington, D.C.: U.S. Department of Education, National Center for Education Statistics, 1991.

Rumberger, Russell W., "Dropping Out of High School: The Influence of Race, Sex, and Family Background," *American Educational Review Journal*, Vol. 20, No. 2, 1983, pp. 199–220.

Schneider, Barbara, and James S. Coleman, *Parents, Their Children, and Schools*, Boulder, Colo.: Westview Press, 1993.

Simons, Janet M., Belva Finlay, and Alice Yang, *The Adolescent and Young Adult Fact Book*, Washington, D.C.: Children's Defense Fund, 1991.

Steinberg, Laurence, Julie D. Elmen, and Nina S. Mounts, "Authoritative Parenting, Psychosocial Maturity, and Academic Success Among Adolescents," *Child Development*, Vol. 60, 1989, pp. 1424–1436.

Stevenson, David L., and David P. Baker, "The Family-School Relation and the Child's School Performance," *Child Development*, Vol. 58, 1987, pp. 1348–1357.

Uhlenberg, Peter, and David Eggebeen, "The Declining Well-Being of American Adolescents," *The Public Interest*, 1986, pp. 25–38.

U.S. Department of Education, National Center for Education Statistics, *Trends in Academic Achievement*, Washington, D.C.: U.S. Government Printing Office, 1991.

U.S. Department of Education, National Center for Education Statistics, *Digest of Education Statistics 1993*, Washington, D.C.: U.S. Government Printing Office, 1993.

Wagenaar, Theodore C., "What Do We Know About Dropping Out of High School?" *Research in the Sociology of Education and Socialization*, Vol. 7, 1987, pp. 161–190.

Wehlage, Gary G., and Robert A. Rutter, "Dropping Out: How Much Do Schools Contribute to the Problem?" *Teachers College Record*, Vol. 87, No. 3, 1986, pp. 374–392.

Wilson, W. J., *The Truly Disadvantaged: The Inner City, the Underclass, and Public Policy*, Chicago, Ill.: The University of Chicago Press, 1987.

Zajonc, Robert, "Family Configuration and Intelligence," *Science*, Vol. 192, 1976, pp. 227–236.

Zill, Nicholas, "Trends in Family Life and School Performance," paper presented at the Annual Meeting of the American Sociological Association, Pittsburgh, Pa., August 1992.

Zill, Nicholas, and Carolyn C Rogers, "Recent Trends in the Well-Being of Children in the United States and their Implications for Public Policy," in Andrew J. Cherlin (ed.), *The Changing American*

Family and Public Policy, Washington, D.C.: The Urban Institute Press, 1988.